FOUNDATION OF NURSING BSC NURSING 1ST YEAR

PREVIOUS YEAR NURSING CHAPTER WISE SOLVED QUESTION PAPERS

RUTWIK UPENDRA BHALSHANKAR

ISBN 979-888530512-9

Contents

CHAPTER ONE

UNIT 1: INTRODUCTION

SHORT ANSWER QUESTION

Q 1 . Define of health.

= Health Traditionally health was defined in terms of the presence or absence of disease.

The World Health Organization (WHO) (1948) takes a more holistic view of health. Its constitution defines health as “a state of complete physical, mental, and social well-being, and not merely the absence of disease or infirmity.”

Q 2. Health illness continuum

= Health–Illness Continua Health–illness continua (grids or graduated scales) can be used to measure a person’s perceived level of wellness. Health and illness or disease can be viewed as the opposite ends of a health continuum.

From a high level of health a person’s condition can move through good health, normal health, poor health, and extremely poor health, eventually to death. People move back and forth within this continuum day by day. There is no distinct boundary across which people move from health to illness or from illness back to health.

DUNN’S HIGH-LEVEL WELLNESS GRID

Dunn (1959) described a health grid in which a health axis and

an environmental axis intersect. The grid demonstrates the interaction of the environment with the illness–wellness continuum

The health axis extends from peak wellness to

death, and the environmental axis extends from very favourable to

very unfavourable. The intersection of the two axes forms four quadrants of health and wellness:

1. High-level wellness in a favourable environment. An example is a

person who implements healthy lifestyle behaviours and has the

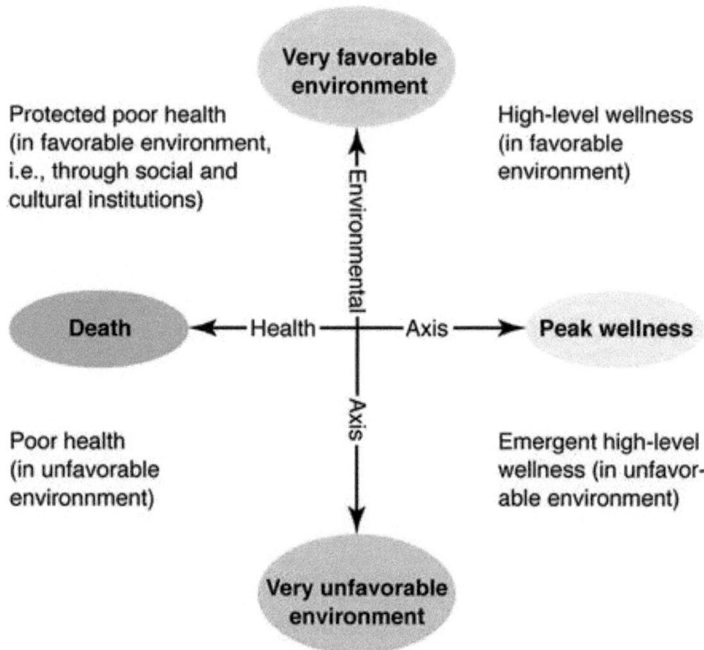

Health illness continuum

biopsychosocial, spiritual, and economic resources to support this lifestyle.

2. Emergent high-level wellness in an unfavourable environment.

An example is a woman who has the knowledge to implement healthy lifestyle practices but does not implement adequate self-care practices because of family responsibilities, job demands, or other factors.

3. Protected poor health in a favourable environment. An example is an ill person (e.g., one with multiple fractures or severe hypertension) whose needs are met by the health care system and who has access to appropriate medications, diet, and health care instruction.

4. Poor health in an unfavourable environment. An example is a young child who is starving in a drought-stricken country.

Q 3. Impact of illness on patient and family

= Effects of Illness Illness brings about changes in both the involved individual and in the family. The changes vary depending on the nature, severity, and duration of the illness, attitudes associated with the illness by the client and others, the financial demands, the lifestyle changes incurred, adjustments to usual roles, and so on.

IMPACT ON THE CLIENT Ill:

- clients may experience behavioral and emotional changes, changes in self-concept and body image, and lifestyle changes.
- Behavioral and emotional changes associated with short-term illness are generally mild and short lived. The individual, for example, may become irritable and lack the energy or desire to interact in the usual fashion with family members or friends
- Certain illnesses can also change the client's body image or physical appearance, especially if there is severe scarring or loss of a limb or sense organ.
- The client's self-esteem and self-concept may also be affected. Many factors can play a part in low self-esteem and a disturbance in self-concept: loss of body parts and function, pain,

disfigurement, dependence on others, unemployment, financial problems, inability to participate in social functions, strained relationships with others, and spiritual distress.

- Illness also often necessitates a change in lifestyle. In addition to participating in treatments and taking medications, the ill person may need to change diet, activity and exercise, and rest and sleep patterns.

IMPACT ON THE FAMILY :

A person's illness affects not only the person who is ill but also the family or significant others. The kind of effect and its extent depend chiefly on three factors: (1) the member of the family who is ill, (2) the seriousness and length of the illness, and (3) the cultural and social customs the family follows. The changes that can occur in the family include the following:

- Role changes
- Task reassignments and increased demands on time
- Increased stress due to anxiety about the outcome of the illness for the client and conflict about unaccustomed responsibilities
- Financial problems
- Loneliness as a result of separation and pending loss
- Change in social customs.

Q 4. Enlist factors influencing health

= Various factors affect a person's health, and medical professionals classify them as internal and external. Internal factors -- also known as hereditary factors or acquired elements -- include smoking and personal diet or eating habits. External factors pertain to the direct outer environment, the geographical location and micro-organisms that could affect an individual's health.

- **Lifestyle and Health**

Lifestyle -- or a typical way of life, as health specialists often define it -- could affect an individual's health and life expectancy. An imbalanced diet or bad eating habits might cause a person to develop chronic diseases, such as diabetes and hypertension, down the road

- . A sedentary lifestyle -- or one with little exercise -- also might not foster good health and physical fitness. Other habits that could adversely affect a person's metabolism include consuming too much saturated fat and starch, abusing alcohol and using illicit drugs, such as cocaine and heroin. Obesity also causes an individual to experience health problems and could lead to diseases and risky conditions including high cholesterol, diabetes and heart disease.

Smoking and Imbalanced Diet

- **Smoking** adversely affects a person's metabolism and life expectancy. According to Dr. Gavin Petrie, cigarettes contain more than 4,000 chemical compounds and at least 400 toxic substances. The most damaging substances in cigarettes include tar, which causes cancer; nicotine, an additive that increases cholesterol levels in the body; and carbon monoxide, which reduces oxygen in the body.
- **An imbalanced diet** -- the kind that results from eating high-calorie, high saturated fats and low-fiber food -- also could have a negative impact on a person's health. For example, fast food often contains higher calories and highly saturated fats that the body does not need. A high calorie diet and low-exercise lifestyle will be harmful to the body over time.

Natural Habitat

- An individual's natural habitat -- the house or apartment where the person lives -- also can affect an individual's health. People who live close to manufacturing facilities or industrial settings are more likely to be exposed to chemicals and other hazardous substances -- such as nuclear residue, asbestos and radioactive materials -- that companies use in the production of goods.

Work Environment

- Occupational pollution -- the other name for workplace pollution -- also can affect an individual's health. For example, workers could suffer from the extreme noise that production equipment generates or harsh chemicals used in cleaning processes. The skin and lungs are the most vulnerable to these effects. Dermatitis -- also known as skin inflammation -- can be caused by detergents and certain rubber chemicals. Inhaling flour or other substances used in bakeries, for example, might cause asthma.

Q 5. Hospice care

= **Hospice** care is a type of care and philosophy of care that focuses on the palliation of a chronically ill, terminally ill or seriously ill patient's pain and symptoms, and attending to their emotional and spiritual needs.

- Hospice care seeks to improve the quality of life and wellbeing of adults and children with a life-limiting or terminal illness, helping them live as fully as they can for the precious time they have
- left. It aspires to be accessible to all who could benefit and reflect personal preferences and needs.
- The modern concept of hospice includes palliative care for the incurably ill given in such institutions as hospitals or nursing

homes, but also care provided to those who would rather spend their last months and days of life in their own homes.

- The first modern hospice care was created by Cicely Saunders in 1967.
- Hospice care is for people with a life expectancy of 6 months or less (if the illness runs its normal course). If you live longer than 6 months, you can still get hospice care, as long as the hospice medical director or other hospice doctor recertifies that you're terminally ill.
- Hospice care is appropriate when a person will no longer benefit from curative treatment and life expectancy is approximately six months if the disease runs its normal course.
- Hospice care is free for everyone, and is provided for however long it is needed, which could be days, weeks or even months.

- **Hospice services**

- Hospices provide a range of services which include:
- pain and symptom control
- psychological and social support
- rehabilitation
- complementary therapies, such as massage and aromatherapy
- counselling
- spiritual care
- practical and financial advice
- support in bereavement.

CHAPTER TWO

UNIT 2: NURSING AS A PROFESSION

SHORT ANSWER QUESTION

Q 1. Nursing as a profession

= Nursing is gaining recognition as a profession. A profession has been defined as an occupation that requires extensive education or a calling that requires special knowledge, skill, and preparation.

A profession is generally distinguished from other kinds of occupations by

(a) its requirement of prolonged, specialized training to acquire a body of knowledge pertinent to the role to be performed;

(b) orientation of the individual toward service, either to a community or to an organization;

(c) ongoing research;

(d) a code of ethics;

(e) autonomy; and

(f) a professional organization.

A services offered by a profession are based on specialised knowledge and skills that have been developed in scientific skills that have been developed in scientific and learned manner.

A profession should be :

- **Intellectual**
- **Scientific**
- **Essential**

- **Self governing**
- **Service oriented**
- **Provide personal development**
- **Economical security for its members.**

Professional nursing is a service promoted to the promotion of human and social welfare . Nursing helps to attain this objectives by applying scientific knowledge and skills to the service which include caring for the sink and injured , promotion and restoration of health and prevention of diseases .

These service are provided by maintaining good interpersonal relationship with medical and paramedical who are interrelated with the health care .

Nursing is now emerged as a profession and nursing practice has greatly changed in these years. Now a days nursing includes a wide range of activities .

Q 2. Functions of nurse.

= Nursing is now emerged as a profession and nursing practice has greatly changed in these years. Now a days nursing includes a wide range of activities, but basically a,

Nurse has to do following functions :

1 Caregiver

The caregiver role has traditionally included those activities that

assist the client physically and psychologically while preserving the

client's dignity. The required nursing actions may involve full care for

the completely dependent client

2.Communicator

Communication is integral to all nursing roles. Nurses communicate with the client, support persons, other health professionals, and

people in the community.

3.Teacher

As a teacher, the nurse helps clients learn about their health and the health care procedures they need to perform to restore or maintain their health. The nurse assesses the client's learning needs and

readiness to learn, sets specific learning goals in conjunction with

the client

4.Counselor

Counselling is the process of helping a client to recognize and cope

with stressful psychological or social problems, to develop improved

interpersonal relationships, and to promote personal growth. It involves providing emotional, intellectual, and psychological support.

5.Research Consumer

Nurses often use research to improve client care. In a clinical area,

nurses need to (a) have some awareness of the process and language

of research, (b) be sensitive to issues related to protecting the rights of human subjects, (c) participate in the identification of significant

researchable problems, and (d) be a discriminating consumer of research findings.

Some others are :

1. To provide best possible nursing care to the patient.
2. To give medication and treatment prescribed by the doctors efficiently.
3. To observe patient illness and his response to the treatment
4. To prevent any complications.
5. To teach patient and his family regarding the prevention of diseases and promotion of health.
6. To participate in research work, related to health care.

7. To teach and supervise the nursing students and other auxiliary personnel.
8. To provide compressive care to the patient , family, and community by teaching at various levels.
9. To maintain her own physical and mental health.

These are the some functions of nurse to be done at every level .

Q 3. Code of ethics in nursing

= Nursing Codes of Ethics

A code of ethics is a formal statement of a group's ideals and values.

It is a set of ethical principles that (a) is shared by members of the

group, (b) reflects their moral judgments over time, and (c) serves as

a standard for their professional actions. Codes of ethics usually have

higher requirements than legal standards, and they are never lower

than the legal standards of the profession. Nurses are responsible for

being familiar with the code that governs their practice.

International, national, and state nursing associations have established codes of ethics. The International Council of Nurses (ICN)

first adopted a code of ethics in 1953,

THE ICN CODE

The ICN Code of Ethics for Nurses has four principal elements that

outline the standards of ethical conduct.

ELEMENTS OF THE CODE

1. Nurses and People

The nurse's primary professional responsibility is to people requiring nursing care.

In providing care, the nurse promotes an environment in

which the human rights, values, customs and spiritual beliefs of the individual, family and community are respected.

The nurse ensures that the individual receives accurate, sufficient and timely information in a culturally appropriate manner on which to base consent for care and related treatment. The nurse holds in confidence personal information and uses judgement in sharing this information.

The nurse shares with society the responsibility for initiating and supporting action to meet the health and social needs of the public, in particular those of vulnerable populations.

The nurse advocates for equity and social justice in resource allocation, access to health care, and other social and economic services.

The nurse demonstrates professional values such as respectfulness, responsiveness, compassion, trustworthiness, and integrity.

2. Nurses and Practice

The nurse carries personal responsibility and accountability for nursing practice, and for maintaining competence by continual learning.

The nurse maintains a standard of personal health such that the ability to provide care is not compromised.

The nurse uses judgement regarding individual competence when accepting and delegating responsibility.

The nurse at all times maintains standards of personal conduct which reflect well on the profession and enhance public confidence.

The nurse, in providing care, ensures that use of technology and scientific advances are compatible with the safety, dignity and rights of people.

The nurse strives to foster and maintain a practice culture promoting ethical behaviour and open dialogue.

3. Nurses and the Profession

The nurse assumes the major role in determining and implementing acceptable standards of clinical nursing practice, management, research and education.

The nurse is active in developing a core of research-based professional knowledge.

The nurse is active in developing and sustaining a core of professional values.

The nurse, acting through the professional organization, participates in creating and maintaining safe, equitable social and economic working conditions in nursing.

The nurse practices to sustain and protect the natural environment and is aware of its consequences on health.

The nurse contributes to an ethical organisational environment and challenges unethical practices and settings.

4. Nurses and Co-workers

The nurse sustains a co-operative relationship with coworkers in nursing and other fields.

The nurse takes appropriate action to safeguard individuals, families and communities when their health is endangered by a co-worker or any other person.

The nurse takes appropriate action to support and guide co-workers to advance ethical conduct.

Q 5. Qualities of nurse

= Nursing is a career which call for many qualities .

Miss Florence nightingle the founder of modern nursing mention in her note qualities and characteristics of nurse . She says " a nurse must be no gossips ,vein talker, be strict sober and honest out more than she must be devoted women , she must have respect for her calling.

To become a good nurse person must posses considerable intelligence, a good education, healthy physique, good manner an even temper a sympathetic temperament and willing hands.

Some essential qualities of nurse are :

1. She should be honest and loyal
2. She should be obedient .
3. She should cultivate the habit of observation .
4. Should love for fellow men.
5. Should sympathy, empathy, tact, and poise.
6. Should have adjustability.
7. Should have patience and sense of humor.
8. Should have physically and mentally fit .
9. Should have sense of responsibilities..
10. She should be good communicator.
11. She should be knowledgeable
12. She should be confident.
13. She should be good listener.

CHAPTER THREE

UNIT 3: HOSPITAL ADMISSION AND DISCHARGE

SHORT ANSWER QUESTION

Q1. Define Admission and ways of admission.

= **Def** : Admission of patient means to hospitalise the patient for observation, investigation, and treatment for the disease he/she is suffering from.

Two way's of admission :

1. **Emergency admission** : The patient is admitted in acute condition requiring immediate treatment. Patient may come to hospital by ambulance, or automobile e.g heart attack, accident , stroke, burn, labor pain
2. **Routine admission** : In this type of the patient are admitted for investigations and medical or surgical treatment is given accordingly. E.g – Patient with a diabetes, hypertensions , hernia.

Q 2. Admission procedure / steps of admission.

= **Def :** Admission of patient means to hospitalise the patient for observation, investigation, and treatment for the disease he/she is suffering from.

There are different steps of admission in hospital. Some stapes are as follows:

1. Meet and receive the patient .
2. Verify the patient data by checking the record sheet, chart.
3. Introduce to immediate person.
4. Assist patient to treatment area.
5. Ask the patient to change cloths into hospital gown if necessary.
6. Care of valuables .

1 . Meet and receive the patient:

Patient come to out patient department after medical examination by doctors, he /she give an indoor case paper and send to the ard with male or female servant . If patient is unable to walk send the patient on wheel chair ,stretcher which is available to respective ward. Seriously ill patients must be left in the hands of trained person.

2 . Verify the patient data by checking the record sheet, chart.

Fill the document or data which is necessary, i.e Name in full ,Age, Occupation, Address , Name and address of relatives , if patient is child ask information to parents .

3 . Introduce to immediate person

Seriously ill patients must be left in the hands of trained person.

4 . Assist patient to treatment area :

Assist patient for medical examination i.e Obsrve patient general conditions, facial expression, skin colour, any deformities which is easily observe, temperature, pulse, and respiration and record it on temperature chart.

5 . Ask the patient to change cloths into hospital gown if necessary

6 . Care of valuables:

Dirty cloths of patient should be send home with a relatives for washing. F patient is alone then they are numbered and label and kept in store. Give at time of discharge.

Any valuables such as jewellery, mobile phones or important documents put in a envelope. And left it in a safe place.

Q 3 . Unit and it's preparation

= Unit and it's preparation It is a place where the patient is kept during hospital stay. The admitting department notifies the unit prior to the patients arrival so that room /bed can be prepared.

Unit and it's preparation Prepare the treatment table, Ensure all the equipment are completed, Check ventilation, Ensure patient privacy.

Q 4 . Role of nurse in admission process

= Role and Responsibilities of Nurse in admission procedure , Nurse should deal every effort to be friendly and courteous with the patient and family members, Make proper observation of patients condition

Orient patient and relatives regarding hospital polices, Deal with patient carefully who is suffering from communicable disease or illness. Isolate if necessary , Patients valuables and clothes should be handed over to relatives with proper recording.

Q 5. Nurses Responsibility in Discharge PREPARATION FOR DISCHARGE

= Planning in the beginning. Nurses Responsibility in Discharge PREPARATION FOR DISCHARGE Planning in the beginning. Plan for rehabilitation and follow-up need. Teach nursing procedures to be continued at home, get it's practice done. Arrangement for transport.

See doctor's written order. Explanations. Hand over personal belongings. Check and receive any hospital property. Confirm bill paid. Inform other departments regarding discharge Arrange transport. DAMA:- check consent

Nurses Responsibility in Discharge AFTER DISCHARGE Documentation. Care of patient's room and articles

Nurses responsibility in MLC Discharge Check for medico legal history. Notify medical officer in charge. Abscond cases immediately contact medical officer in charge. Maintain all documents in a proper manner. Take in written handing over and taking of articles. Never discharge patient without written order by physician.

Checklist M E T H O D

Checklist M = MEDICATION E = ENVIRONMENT T = TREATEMENT H = HEALTH TEACHING O = OUT PATIENT REFFERAL D = DIET

Q 6 . Types of discharge

= **Definition** "Discharge of patient from the hospital means, reliving a person from hospital setting, who admitted as an inpatient in that hospital".

Types of Discharge

1. PLANNED DISCHARGE:- Patient completes the initial, actual management in the hospital and now he or she need not to be under direct supervision of that hospital.'

2. DAMA/LAMA: Discharge/Leave Against Medical Advice

3. TRANSFER: Transfer to other unit or hospital

4. ABSCOND: Abscond from Hospital

5. REFFERAL : Referred for further management Consent for DAMA I am leaving the hospital ward against medical advice. Doctor explained me about my disease condition and ill effects of discharge against medical advice. Doctors and Nursing staffs will not be responsible for any ill effects happening after my departure". Name of the patient / relative :- Relation:- Signature:- Date :- Time:-

CHAPTER FOUR

UNIT 4: COMMUNICATION AND NURSE PATIENT RELATIONSHIP

SHORT ANSWER QUESTION

Q1 Importance of communication

= To some communication is the exchange of information between two or more people, in other sense the exchange of ideas or thought.

In simple words communication is the reciprocal exchange of ideas, information, beliefs, feelings and attitude between person or among groups of person: talking, listening, writing, reading, painting, dancing, storytelling are the various means of exchanging information

The term communication is derived from latin word "communicare" means to share or to impart

Webster's New Collegiate dictionary defines communication as a process by which information is exchanged between individuals through a common system of symbols, signs or behaviour

- To transfer information between all classes of employees to have a common understanding among them

- To interpret and adopt policies in the organization
- To induce motivation, co-operation and co-ordination in the employees
- To improve employer- employee relationships
- To recruit, elect, train and develop the personnel in the organization
- To boost the group morale of the workers
- To ensure job satisfaction
- To inform the community of the services available in the organization
- To prepare the personnel and the public for a change process
- To improve the relation with the government and other agencies
- To get the feedback from the personnel and the public for improvement

Q 2 Levels of communication

=

To some communication is the exchange of information between two or more people, in other sense the exchange of ideas or thought.

In simple words communication is the reciprocal exchange of ideas, information, beliefs, feelings and attitude between person or among groups of person: talking, listening, writing, reading, painting, dancing, storytelling are the various means of exchanging information

The level of communications are as follows :

1. Intrapersonal communication:

- It is a powerful form of communication that occurs within an individual
- This level of communication is also called self talk, self verbalization and inner thought
- People's thoughts strongly influence perceptions, feelings, behavior and self concept

- Nurses should be aware of the nature and content of their own thinking and try to replace negative, self defeating thoughts with positive assertions.
- Nurses and clients can use intrapersonal communication to develop self awareness and a positive self concept that will enhance appropriate self expression.

2.. Interpersonal communication:

- It is one to one interaction between the nurse and another person that often occurs face to face
- It is the level most frequently used in nursing situations and lies at the heart of nursing practice
- It takes place within a social context and includes all the symbols and cues used to give and receive meaning
- Nurses work with people who have different opinions, experiences, values and belief systems so meaning must be validated or mutually negotiated between participants
- Meaningful IC results in exchange of ideas, problem solving, expression of feelings, decision making, goal accomplishment, team building and personal growth.

3. Transpersonal communication:

- It is interaction that occurs within a person's spiritual domain
- Many person use prayer, meditation, guided reflection, religious rituals or other means to communicate with their higher power
- Nurses who value the importance of human spirituality often use this form of communication with clients and for themselves

4. SMALL GROUP COMMUNICATION:

- It is interaction that occurs when a small number of persons meet together

- This type of communication is usually goal directed and requires an understanding of group dynamics
- Small groups are more effective when they are a workable size, have a appropriate meeting place, suitable seating arrangements and cohesiveness and commitment among group members.
- Furthermore Darley (2002) suggests that there are two main principles that are important to ensure effective communication and working relationships between people in any group.

5. PUBLIC COMMUNICATION:

- It is interaction with an audience
- Nurses have opportunities to speak with groups of consumers about health related topics, present scholarly work to colleagues at conferences, or lead classroom discussions with peers or students
- It requires special adaptation in eye contact, gestures, voice inflection and use of media materials to communicate message effectively
- Effective PC increases audience knowledge about health related topics, health issues, and other issues important to the nursing profession.

Q 3. Types of communication

=

To some communication is the exchange of information between two or more people, in other sense the exchange of ideas or thought.

In simple words communication is the reciprocal exchange of ideas, information, beliefs, feelings and attitude between person or among groups of person: talking, listening, writing, reading, painting, dancing, storytelling are the various means of exchanging information .

Types of communicartion are as follows :

BASED ON RELATIONSHIP:

Formal communication: It is the communication between officials on various positions in any organisation or institution. E.g. between nursing superintendent and staff nurse.

- It occurs officially e.g. in the hospital, company, college, school etc.
- It occurs in formal way i.e. formal language is used and it is done for the welfare of organisation
- It involves transmitting official message within or outside the organisation
- Line of authority and unity of command are maintained
- It involves also communication between the departments

Informal communication: It is the communication between two people may be in social system or in organization. E.g. interaction between two close friends.

- It is very simple
- This is very informal talk with the people e.g. gossiping, back biting etc
- There is no formality in delivering the message among people

BASED UPON FLOW:

- **Upward communication:** Communication occurs from bottom to the top. It may be in the form of suggestions, complaints, report etc. it can be verbal or in written form.
- E.g. application for leave, suggestions from staff nurses to nursing superintendent for improving the quality care in hospital, written complaint by staff nurse to the director regarding misbehaviour of the nursing superintendent

Downward communication: It is the communication which occurs from top to bottom such as communication from superior to subordinates.

- E.g. from nursing superintendent to staff nurses
- Downward communication is done to:
- Convey information (in the form of circular), instructions (policy, rule and regulations), orders (transfers, promotion etc) which are related to organizational activities and policies.
- E.g. information conveyed by president to nursing superintendent regarding hospital policies, promotion of employees etc.

Horizontal communication: The communication flows horizontally among same hierarchical levels. E.g. communication among colleagues, communication among lecturers, among staff nurses, among clinical instructors.

- This kind of communication helps to improve the understanding among groups.

One way communication: It is the flow of communication from sender to receiver only. It always flows in one direction.

MESSAGE
SENDER ------------->>> RECEIVER
NO FEEDBACK

- There is no feedback i.e. sender will not receive response from receiver. No participation of receiver.
- E.g. lecture delivered by teacher in class room

Two way communication: It is the flow of communication from sender to receiver and again from receiver to sender. There is participation of the receiver or listener. It flows in two directions i.e. forward and backward. Here the message passes from sender to receiver and from receiver to sender in the form of feedback. E.g. group discussion. Receiver may add something to raise questions. It involves active learning.

MESSAGE

SENDER RECEIVER
FEEDBACK
OTHERS:

- **Visual communication:** In this communication message is conveyed using symbols in the form of charts, maps, posters, painting etc. also known as symbolic communication.
- E.g. displayed models in exhibition, displayed posters on the wall
- **Telecommunication:** It is the process of communicating in distant places with help of electromagnetic appliances
- E.g. television, radio, internet etc.

Q 4. Barriers of communication

= To some communication is the exchange of information between two or more people, in other sense the exchange of ideas or thought.

In simple words communication is the reciprocal exchange of ideas, information, beliefs, feelings and attitude between person or among groups of person: talking, listening, writing, reading, painting, dancing, storytelling are the various means of exchanging information .

The barriers of communications are as following .

Physiological barriers:

- Difficulty in hearing
- Difficulty in vision
- Difficulty in expressions

- **Psychological barriers:**

- Emotional disturbance (crisis, anxiety, severe stress)
- Neurosis (a relatively mild mental illness that is not caused by organic disease, involving symptoms of stress - depression, anxiety but not a radical loss of touch with reality)

- Level of intelligence
- Fear
- Ego centricity, superior or inferior complex
- **Environmental barrier:**
- Lack of ventilation
- Lack of light
- Extreme temperature
- Extreme noise
- Lack of privacy
- Congestion etc

- **Organizational barriers :** Policy, Rules & Regulation, Complex organization ,Status & Position
- **Cultural barriers:**

- Level of knowledge and understanding
- Personality traits
- Beliefs
- Religion
- Attitude
- Language
- **Semantic Barriers (Problems of language) :** Badly expressed message, Jargon language (the language, especially the vocabulary, peculiar to a particular trade, profession, or group: medical jargon. Any talk or writing that one does not understand), Faulty translation
- **Mechanical Barrier :** Non-availability of proper equipments, Presence of defective machineries, Interruption or power failure
- **Situational factors:** Stress. Pain and discomfort, fear and anxiety, dyspnoea, fatigue, hearing impairment

Q 5. Communication skills

=

To some communication is the exchange of information between two or more people, in other sense the exchange of ideas or thought.

In simple words communication is the reciprocal exchange of ideas, information, beliefs, feelings and attitude between person or among groups of person: talking, listening, writing, reading, painting, dancing, storytelling are the various means of exchanging information

Confidence: Confidence is very important for developing and maintaining a trust with others. Nurse will be confident if she has up to date knowledge, skilful and as well as having the self concept.

- **Critical thinker:** Nurse must have this quality for the effective communication. She must collect the information, analyse it, and then interpret it. Nurse must think critically about the message she wants to communicate.
- **Analytical:** Means ability to examine the impact of message on listener/ recipients. For effective communication nurse must be able to examine the verbal, non verbal response of client.
- **Open mindness:** An open minded communication will explore the information by entering in the situation
- **Active listener:** Is the best quality of a good communication. This can be done by nodding the head, maintaining eye contact, saying “Yes” “No” in between the conversation
- **Empathetic:** Empathy means perceiving the clients feelings. Being empathetic enable the nurse to help the client. Simultaneously, client also develops trust on the nurse.
- **Honest:** Honesty is very important in any of communication whether it is formal, informal, interpersonal or intrapersonal.
- **Confidentiality:** To keep the information secret and use it for the particular purpose (welfare of client) confidentiality is important skill. Nurse must maintain confidentiality of client (psychiatry client, AIDS, HBS +ve). She must maintain client’s right to privacy and share the information professionally for providing best care and treatment.
- **Knowledgeable:** Having a professional knowledge is important skill in effective communication. Knowledge regarding what to

ask and how to ask is also essential. Along with this, knowledge about the clients values, perception, beliefs, feelings, developmental age, culture, ethnic group is very important to initiate communication.

- **Systematic:** Being systematic is important because good communicators tend to seek and provide information in an organised and focussed way. Communication must be proceeded from simple to complex manner.
- **Tactfulness:** Is the pivotal quality for effective communication. How to convey message and get response is the essential quality of a good communicator.

Q 6. Modes of communication

= To some communication is the exchange of information between two or more people, in other sense the exchange of ideas or thought.

In simple words communication is the reciprocal exchange of ideas, information, beliefs, feelings and attitude between person or among groups of person: talking, listening, writing, reading, painting, dancing, storytelling are the various means of exchanging information

Mode of communications

Mode means the way by which communication occurs. The message can be sent verbally (talking) or non verbally (gestures).

- **Mode of communication:** There are two modes of communication i.e. verbal and non verbal. These are described as follows:

1. **Verbal communication:**

- It includes all the words, the speaker speaks.
- Talking is most common activity.
- Source/ sender communicates beliefs, values, perception, meaning, interest and also understands it.

- The various aspects of verbal communication are as follows:

- **Vocabulary:**

- For the effective communication, sender as well as receiver should have similarity in language understanding.
- Because person belonging to different culture, ethnic group may find difficulty to understand and interpret the message.

- **Pacing:**

- Using pause at right time in order to make communication effective.
- Sender must speak slowly, clearly and use pauses to stress particular point.
- Giving pause helps the listener to understand.
- If sender talks rapidly, using pauses at awkward time, speaking very slowly, using slurred speech can convey an unintended message.
- Even long pause, shifting to another topic may give wrong impression of telling lie.
- **Denotative and connotative meaning:** The denotative meaning is shared by individuals who use common language. E.g. Punjabi people using language "Punjabi".
- Connotative meaning is the interpretation of words, meaning, influenced by the thoughts, feelings or ideas people have about the word.

E.g. families who are told a loved one is in serious condition may believe that death is near, but to nurses serious may simply describe the nature of the illness.

- **Simplicity:**
- For effective verbal communication sender must use simple language, easily understood words, brevity and complete words.

- Message conveyed by nurse should be so simple that it could be interpreted easily by a layman. Thus nurse should avoid using medical terminologies.

- E.g. instead of saying "your leg will be cut". It can be stated as "due to gangrene formation part of lower limb will be cut by keeping you unconscious.

- **Clarity and brevity:** Conveyed message should be very simple and clear, short to minimize confusion. Brevity means using few necessary words for making message easily understood.
- **Timing and relevance:**

- If the message conveyed is in simple language, less time will be consumed for understanding it.
- Even the timing for interaction also matters. E.g. if client is undergoing an appendectomy in emergency situation. It is not appropriate time to collect information regarding his family, interest etc.
- Relevance of message is equally important. For e.g. discussing the complications of surgery is irrelevant for client admitted in medicine ward with typhoid fever.
- Message should be related to the person's interest and concerns.

- **Adaptability:**

- Spoken message should be modified as per client's behavioural clues. This adjustment is known as adaptability.
- For e.g. nurse must know how to speak and express her gestures while interacting with an elated client or depressed client.
- As per clients behaviour nurse should alter her tone of speech and expression. For e.g. on a death of client in ward nurse should express sad expressions.

2. **Non verbal communication:**

- Non verbal communication includes use of body languages such as gestures, gait, use of touch, physical appearance.
- It helps in expression of feelings better than the spoken words.
- Observing and interpreting client's non verbal behaviour efficiently is an essential skill for effective communication.

- **Physical appearance:**

- Clothing, dressing, grooming, and hygiene provide information regarding social, financial status, culture, religion, group association and even the self concept.
- Change in clients dressing sense gives a clue regarding his health status. Nurse can validate this by asking the client.

- **Body language, posture and gait:**

- "Actions speak more than words" is a well known saga.
- Body movements, posture, gait of client depicts clients current mood, health status as well as about his self concept. Erect posture, purposeful stride reveals a healthy well being.
- Whereas slouched posture and a slow shuffling gait suggests depression or physical discomfort.
- Tense posture, rapid movements reflects anxiety. After observing body language, nurse verifies her interpretation by asking to client.
- **Physical appearance:**
- Clothing, dressing, grooming, and hygiene provide information regarding social, financial status, culture, religion, group association and even the self concept.
- Change in clients dressing sense gives a clue regarding his health status. Nurse can validate this by asking the client.

- **Body language, posture and gait:**

- "Actions speak more than words" is a well known saga.

- Body movements, posture, gait of client depicts clients current mood, health status as well as about his self concept. Erect posture, purposeful stride reveals a healthy well being.
- Whereas slouched posture and a slow shuffling gait suggests depression or physical discomfort.
- Tense posture, rapid movements reflects anxiety. After observing body language, nurse verifies her interpretation by asking to client.
- **Eye contact:**
- Eye contact maintenance during interaction shows the confidence and willingness of client to listen.
- Lack of eye contact may reflect anxiety, discomfort in communication.
- Even eye movements reveal feelings and emotions.
- Wide eyes express frankness, terror.
- Raised upper eyelids reveal displeasure.
- Constant staring may be associated with hatred or coldness.

- **Observable autonomic physiologic responses:**

- Such as increased respiration, sweating, pupil dilation, blushing, paleness also reflects client's mental as well as physical health status.
- Physical characteristics such as height, weight, physique, complexion, blueness of lip, nail reflects the lack of oxygen in tissues.
- Weight and muscle tone reflects the weakness level.
- Paleness reflects anaemia/ anxiety level of client.

- **Voice related behaviour:**

- Voice tone (happy-good), pitch level (high pitch – aggressiveness, hyperactivity), intensity of voice (high in pain), stuttering (in anxiety), pause (can't express), silence (not interesting),

- **Facial expression:** Frown, smile, yawn, pursed lip, tongue movement.

Q 7. Factors influencing communication process

= **Developmental / Age of the client** influence the communication:

- As per the developmental stage of life, needs of client vary.
- For example: A child can learn effectively through a story or by using dolls, games. Adolescent needs more explanations as he/ she is curious.
- With age body changes also occur. Such as vision problem, hearing problem etc.
- knowledge of clients developmental stage helps the nurse how to and what message to be conveyed him.

◦ **Gender:**

- Male and female communication patterns tend to differ which can sometimes create barriers of communication
- Male communicate to achieve goals, establish individual status and authority. They typically prefer to talk about topics that do not expose personal feelings
- Females communicate to build connections with others. Women enjoy discussing feelings and personal issues.
- **Values and perceptions:**
- Every human being perceives and interprets message according to his personality trait, values, experience.
- It is very important for the nurse to understand the client's values and perception.
- She can verify it from client to avoid creating barriers in the nurse client relationship.
- For example : In hospital nurse restricts the visitors entry to avoid infection occurrence but a burn patient may receive it other way i.e. because of defect in her physical appearance, her

family members are not visiting her. Here understanding values and perceptions of client are very important.

- **Personal space:**
- Personal space is the distance maintained by persons in interaction with others.
- Professional nurse maintains good interpersonal relations and by observing client's health status also maintains personal space.
- For example: When a client is emotionally very upset or child is admitted in hospital and is crying. She acts as mother, friend. For a normal client she maintains a professional distance
- **Territoriality:**
- Is a concept of the space and things that an individual considers as belonging to the self.
- For example: As client is admitted in hospital he is getting bed, locker, chair, utensils etc. Client considers all these things as his territories while taking anything from client nurse must sought permission from the client to remove or rearrange or to borrow.
- **Roles and relationships:**
- The role and relationship between sender and receiver affect significantly the communication process.
- A girl will interact differently with her father, teacher, friend, sister, nurse, strange person.
- Thus the content of message, choice of words, sentence structure and tone of voice varies from role to role.
- The nurse who meets a client for first time communicates differently from the nurse who has previously developed a relationship with that client.
- **Environment:**
- A conducive and therapeutic environment is the necessity for the effective communication.
- So the communication should be noise free, well ventilated and have temperature within normal range.
- Lack of privacy, light also affects the communication.
- **Congruence:**

- Is to what extent verbal and non verbal expressions are similar or match to each other.
- Because if nurse's verbal and non verbal message does not match client will loose trust and avoid interacting with a nurse.
- For example while doing care of AIDS patient if nurse is making disgusting expressions client will does not want to disclose his information with nurse.
- **Interpersonal attitudes:**
- Attitudes reflects the beliefs, thoughts and feelings about people and events.
- Attitude such as caring, warmth, respect and acceptance facilitates communication.
- Thus nurse having such attitude will develop good interpersonal relations with client and colleagues whereas the lack of interest, coldness inhibits the communication and ultimately relationship.

Q 8. Nurse patient relationship

= **Definition** , It is an interaction process in which the nurse fulfils her role by using her professional knowledge and skill in such a way that she is able to help the patient physically, socially and emotionally.

- It is an interaction process between two person in which the nurse offers a series of purposeful activities and practices that are useful to particular patient

Characteristic =

- It is an intellectual and emotional bond between the nurse and client and mainly focussed on the client
- It respects the clients as an individual by:
- Maximizing the client's abilities to participate in decision making
- Considering ethnic and cultural aspects

- Considering family relationships and values
- It respects clients confidentiality and values
- It emphasis on the client's well being
- It is based on the mutual trust, respect and acceptance

.DEVELOPING HELPING RELATIONSHIPS

- Listen actively
- Be honest
- Be genuine and credible
- Be aware of cultural differences
- Maintain client's confidentiality
- Know your roles and your limitations

CHAPTER FIVE

UNIT 5: NURSING PROCESS

SHORT ANSWER QUESTION

Q 1. Levels of critical thinking in Nursing

- = **Def**: Critical thinking is an active, organized, cognitive process used to carefully examine one's thinking and the thinking of others.
- It involves use of the mind in forming conclusions, making decisions, drawing inferences and reflecting.

LEVELS OF CRITICAL THINKING

- **Basic critical thinking:**
- At the basic level of critical thinking a learner trusts that experts have the right answers for every problem.
- Thinking is concrete and based on a set of rules or principles.
- For example, a nurse uses an institutions procedure manual to confirm how to insert a Foleys catheter.
- The student nurse follows the procedure step by step without adjusting the procedure to meet a client's unique needs (eg positioning to accommodate the client's pain or mobility restrictions).
- For basic critical thinkers answers to complex problems are either right or wrong (e.g. there is too much or insufficient air in

the Foleys catheter balloon), and one right answer usually exists for each problem.

- This is an early step in the development of reasoning ability, revealing that the individual has had critical thinking experience.
- Despite the tendency to be governed by others, a person learns to accept the diverse opinions and values of experts (e.g. instructors and staff nurse role models).
- However inexperience, weak competencies and inflexible attitudes can restrict a person's ability to move to the next level of critical thinking.

Complex critical thinking:

- A person begins to detach from authorities and analyze and examine alternatives more independently at the complex level of critical thinking.
- Kataoka yahiro and saylor note that the nurse's best answer to a problem at this level is "It depends".
- The person's thinking abilities and initiative to look beyond expert opinion begin to change.
- A nurse realizes that alternative and perhaps conflicting, solution do exist.
- Consider the case of Mr. Rosen a 36 year old man who underwent hip surgery. The client is having pain but refusing his ordered analgesic. His physician is concerned that the client will not progress as planned, delaying rehabilitation. While discussing the importance of rehabilitation with Mr. Rosen the nurse realizes the client's conviction to avoid taking pain medication. The nurse learns that the client practices meditation at home and decides to discuss this with the client as a pain control option. In complex critical thinking each solution has benefits and risks that the nurse weighs before making a final decision. There are options. Thinking is a willingness to consider deviations from standard protocols or policies when

complex situations develop. Nurses learn a variety of different approaches for the same therapy.

Commitment:

- The third level of critical thinking is commitment.
- The individual anticipates the need to make choices without assistance from others and then assumes accountability for them.
- At this level the nurse does more than just consider the complex alternatives a problem poses.
- At the commitment level, the nurse chooses an action or belief based on the alternatives available and stands by it.
- Sometimes an action may be no action, or the nurse may choose to delay an action until a later time but does so as a result of experience and knowledge. Because the nurse assumes accountability for the decision and a determination of whether it was appropriate.

Q 2 . Define nursing process.

- **= It may be defined as a systematic method of assessing the health status, diagnosing health care needs, formulating a plan of care, initiating the plan and evaluating the effectiveness of the plan.**
- **The term nursing process was introduced by Hall in 1955.**

Q 3 Steps of nursing process.

=It may be defined as a systematic method of assessing the health status, diagnosing health care needs, formulating a plan of care, initiating the plan and evaluating the effectiveness of the plan.

Nursing assessment:

- Nursing assessment is the process of gathering, verifying and communicating data about a client.

- It helps in establishing base line data about client's level of wellness, health practices, past illness and related experiences and health care goals.
- It takes place during the nurse's first encounter with a new patient and continues throughout the nurse patient association.

Steps of nursing process.

Nursing diagnosis:

- Nursing diagnosis is a statement of the potential or actual problem in the client's health status that the nurse is licensed and competent to treat.
- It involves identifying the problems of client, family and significant others. Based upon the nursing assessment, nurse formulates nursing diagnosis.
- **Planning:** In simple words planning is the process of thinking before doing. It involves determination of goals as well as nursing activities required to be undertaken to achieve the desired/ set goals. In nursing , planning involves setting goal, expected outcome, priorities and nursing care to be performed.

- **Implementation:** Implementation follows the planning phase of nursing process. It puts the nursing care plan into actions.
- **Evaluation:** Evaluation is the consequences/ results, outcome of the nursing intervention. It may be positive or negative. It is a formal and systematic procedure of determining the effectiveness of the nursing care given.

Q 3. Nursing care plan.

= A written nursing care plan includes a nursing diagnostic statement, goals, expected outcomes and specific nursing activities and interventions.

- Purposes of care plans:

- The nursing care plan is a written guidance for client care. Nursing care plan identifies and coordinate resources used to deliver nursing care.
- It enhances the continuity of nursing care between nurses in the hospital and community
- Nursing care plan helps in evaluation of care and in determining whether the goals of care have been achieved.

Q 4 . Nursing diagnosis

= DEFINITION:

- In 1990 NANDA adopted an official working definition of nursing diagnosis ".... a clinical judgement about individual, family or community responses to actual and potential health problems/ life processes.
- Nursing diagnosis provides the basis for selection of nursing interventions to achieve outcomes for which the nurse is accountable.

Q 5 . Types of nursing diagnosis.

- = **An actual diagnosis:** Is a client problem that is present at the time of the nursing assessment. Examples are ineffective breathing pattern and anxiety. An actual nursing diagnosis is based on the presence of associated signs and symptoms.
- **A risk nursing diagnosis:** Is a clinical judgement that a problem does not exist but the presence of risk factors indicates that a problem is likely to develop unless nurses intervene. For example all people admitted to a hospital have some possibility of acquiring an infection; however a client with diabetes or a compromised immune system is at higher risk than others. Therefore the nurse would appropriately use the label Risk for infection to describe the client's health status.
- **A wellness diagnosis:** "Describes human responses to level of wellness in an individual, family or community that have a readiness for enhancement. Examples of wellness diagnosis would be Readiness for enhanced spiritual well being or Readiness for enhanced family coping.
- **A possible nursing diagnosis:** Is one in which evidence about a health problem is incomplete or unclear. A possible diagnosis requires more data either to support or to refute. For example an elderly widow who lives alone is admitted to the hospital. The nurse notices that she has no visitors and is pleased with attention and conversation from the nursing staff. Until more data are collected the nurse may write a nursing diagnosis of Possible Social Isolation related to unknown aetiology.
- **A syndrome diagnosis:** Is a diagnosis that is associated with a cluster of other diagnoses. Currently six syndrome diagnoses are on the NANDA International list. Risk for Disuse syndrome, for example may be experienced by long term bedridden clients. Clusters of diagnoses associated with this syndrome include Impaired physical mobility, Risk for Impaired Tissue integrity, Risk for activity intolerance, Risk for constipation, Risk for infection, Risk for injury, Risk for powerlessness, and so on.

Q 6. COMPONENTS OF NURSING DIAGNOSIS

= COMPONENTS OF NURSING DIAGNOSIS :

A nursing diagnosis has three components:

(1) the problem and its definition,

(2) the aetiology, and

(3) the defining characteristics. Each component serves a specific function.

1) Problem (diagnostic label) and definition: The problem statement or diagnostic label describes the client's health problem or response for which nursing therapy is given. It describes the client health status clearly and concisely in a few words. The purpose of the diagnostic label is to direct the formation of client goals and desired outcomes. It may also suggest some nursing interventions.

E.g. knowledge deficit, acute, chronic, ineffective, altered, decreased etc.

2) Aetiology (Related factors and risk factors):

- The aetiology component of nursing diagnosis identifies one or more probable causes of the health problem, gives direction to the required nursing therapy, and enables the nurse to individualize the client's care.
- For example the probable causes of activity intolerance include sedentary lifestyle, generalized weakness and so on. Differentiating among possible causes in the nursing diagnosis is essential because each may require different nursing interventions.

3) Defining characteristics: Defining characteristics are the cluster of sign and symptoms of problem which helps in validating the nursing diagnosis. It includes subjective or objective data.

- Eg: 1. Fluid volume deficit related to decreased oral intake manifested by dry skin and mucous membranes
- 2. Risk for impaired skin integrity related to immobility manifested by redness on sacral region.

Q 7. Difference between medical and nursing diagnosis .

=

Comparison of Nursing & Medical Diagnoses	
Nursing Diagnosis	**Medical Diagnosis**
A clinical judgement concerning an undesirable human response to health conditions/life processes (illnesses or injuries).	A clinical judgement concerning the disease or condition that explains the signs and symptoms of a person's illness or injury.
Names an undesirable human response to a health condition or life process (including illness or injury).	Names a disease, illness or injury.
Names vulnerability to undesirable human responses that could likely happen; 'at risk' diagnoses; 'red flags' to increase awareness that these can be prevented by good nursing practice, e.g. skin breakdown.	Names collaborative problems, that is physiological complications of medical diagnoses, that can be life threatening; 'red flags' that both nurses and doctors watch for and treat collaboratively.
Names motivation and desire for increased well-being; readiness for assistance to enhance specific health behaviours.	Readiness for increased well-being not usually a focus.
Are made for patients and also for patients' family members or care-givers. (Gallagher-Lepak 2014)	Are made only for patients.

Difference between medical and nursing diagnosis .

Q 8. List down any five nursing diagnosis

1. Pain related to surgical procedure as evidence by patient verbalization and pain scale.
2. Disturbed sleep pattern related to the pain as evidence by patient verbalization .
3. Activity intolerance related to pain he is not able to eat as evidence by weakness.
4. Change in nutrition less than body requirements related to lack of appetite .

5. Risk for impaired skin integrity related to immobility manifested by redness on sacral region.
6. Fluid volume deficit related to decrease oral intake manifested by dry skin and mucous membrane and mucous membrane.
7. Knowledge deficit s evidence by patient anxiety and frequent questioning about disease condition.

Q 9 .List down he Types of data and differentiate between subjective and objective data .

=

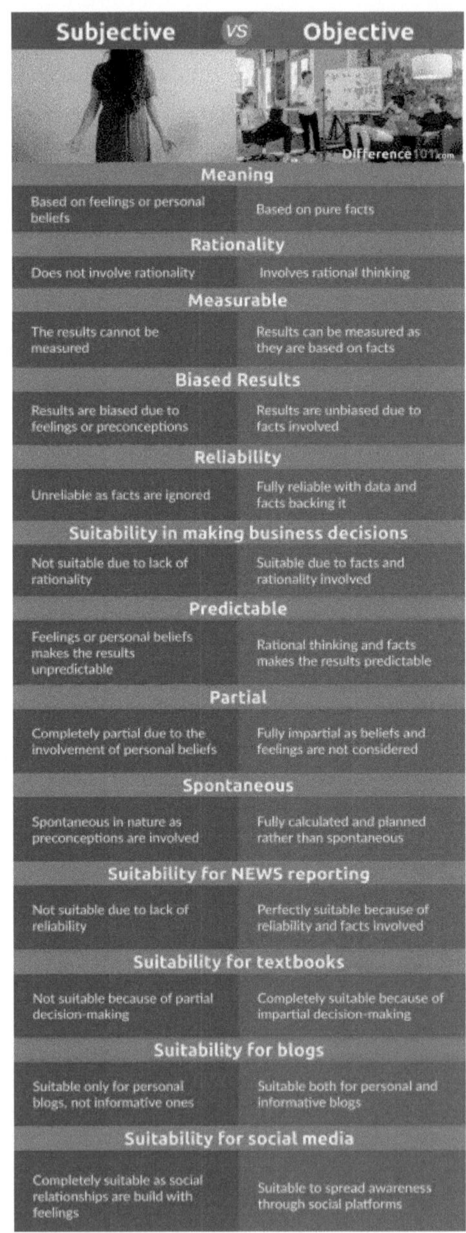

	Subjective	Objective
Meaning	Based on feelings or personal beliefs	Based on pure facts
Rationality	Does not involve rationality	Involves rational thinking
Measurable	The results cannot be measured	Results can be measured as they are based on facts
Biased Results	Results are biased due to feelings or preconceptions	Results are unbiased due to facts involved
Reliability	Unreliable as facts are ignored	Fully reliable with data and facts backing it
Suitability in making business decisions	Not suitable due to lack of rationality	Suitable due to facts and rationality involved
Predictable	Feelings or personal beliefs makes the results unpredictable	Rational thinking and facts makes the results predictable
Partial	Completely partial due to the involvement of personal beliefs	Fully impartial as beliefs and feelings are not considered
Spontaneous	Spontaneous in nature as preconceptions are involved	Fully calculated and planned rather than spontaneous
Suitability for NEWS reporting	Not suitable due to lack of reliability	Perfectly suitable because of reliability and facts involved
Suitability for textbooks	Not suitable because of partial decision-making	Completely suitable because of impartial decision-making
Suitability for blogs	Suitable only for personal blogs, not informative ones	Suitable both for personal and informative blogs
Suitability for social media	Completely suitable as social relationships are build with feelings	Suitable to spread awareness through social platforms

subjective and objective data .

Q 10. Sources of data

= Sources of data are primary or secondary.

- The client is the primary source of data.
- Family members or other support persons, other health professionals, records and reports, laboratory and diagnostic analyses and relevant literature are secondary or indirect sources.
- In fact all sources other than the client are considered secondary sources.
- **Client:** The best source of data is usually the client unless the client is too ill, young or confused to communicate clearly. The client can provide subjective data that no one else can offer.
- **Support people:** Family members, friends and caregivers who know the client well often can supplement or verify information provided by the client. They might convey information about the client's response to illness, the stresses the client was experiencing before the illness, family attitudes on illness and health and the clients home environment.
- **Client records:** Client records include information documented by various health care professionals. Client records also contain data regarding the client's occupation, religion and marital status.
- **Medical records:** (e.g. medical history, physical examination, operative report, progress notes and consultations done by physicians) are often a source of a client's present and past health and illness patterns.
- **Records of therapies** provided by other health professionals, such as social workers, nutritionists, dieticians, or physical therapists help the nurse obtain relevant data not expressed by the client. For example a social agency's report on a client's living conditions or a home health care agency's
- **Laboratory records** also provide pertinent health information. For example the determination of blood glucose level allows

health professionals to monitor the administration of oral hypoglycaemic medications.

- **Health care professionals**: Because assessment is an ongoing process verbal reports from other health care professionals serve as other potential sources of information about a client's health.

- **Literature:** The review of nursing and related literature such as professional journals and reference texts can provide additional information of the database.

CHAPTER SIX

UNIT 6: DOCUMENTATION AND REPORTING

SHORT ANSWER QUESTION

Q 1. Purposes of documentation

= **Documentation:**

- It is the process of communicating in written form about essential facts for the maintenance of continuous history of events over a period of time.
- **Communication:** One of the important purpose of documentation is to communicate the information among health care workers. It is an account of the client's history, present health status, treatment and response to treatment.
- Documentation helps in providing comprehensive nursing care.
- **Legal records:** One of the purpose of documentation is to protect the client as well as health workers. Every client has a right to inform and access the information on chart. Documentation is invaluable for checking the malpractice and also in medico legal cases.
- **Education:** One of the purpose of documentation is to educate/ teach the Medical students. Client's records are used by all disciplines in teaching rounds.

- **Research:** Documentation means written evidence/ proof. Research also needs evidence/ proof. Thus documentation also serves this purpose. For retrospective research, documentation is very important. (e.g. statistical data relating to the frequency of clinical disorders)
- **Audit:** Nursing audit is a way of reviewing the records for the purpose of collecting data. The purpose of auditing is to check quality of care provided. It can be done only if we have written proof i.e. documentation. (it gives a basis for evaluation of the quality and appropriateness of care provided in an institution)

Q 2. Importance of records and reports
= **Records:**

- Records is a clinical, scientific, administrative legal document relating to the nursing care given to individual family and community.
- **Reports:** Reports are oral or written exchange of information shared between nurses or a number of persons. Report is concise and contains pertinent information. Reporting is the communication of information to another individual (or group of individuals).

Importance of records and reports are as follows :
1. Decision making:

- Plays an important role for making decision.
- Based upon the previous data, future planning, even decisions can be made.

2. Planning client care:

- Helpful for planning nursing care to the patients.

3. Communication :

- Important for conveying the information to the employees, employer as well as to the public.

4. Legal documentation:

- Records are very helpful for the legal purposes especially in medico-legal cases.

5. Education :

- Helpful for teaching the nursing as well as medical students.

6. Research :

- Records are the secondary source for data collection.

7. Auditing:

- Auditor needs records for doing the auditing.

8. Quality assurance monitoring:

- Vital Records are used especially for assessing mortality and morbidity rate.

9. Financial billing

10. Accrediting and licensing: Record keeping is basis of good patient care. Thus it should be integral to all practices.

Q 3. Types of records

=

Records:

- Records is a clinical, scientific, administrative legal document relating to the nursing care given to individual family and community.

Types of Records ;

A. Ward Records

- Patient clinical record
- Admission record
- Discharge record
- Census record
- Complaint book
- Movement register
- Visitors record
- Indent book
- Round register
- Attendance record
- Linen book
- Treatment record
- Stock and issue register
- Death register

B. Medical/Nurses Record

- Nurse assessment sheet
- Change of shift record
- Standardized care plan
- Nurses report book
- Nurses progress note
- Treatment chart
- Graphic sheet

C. Student Record

- Application forms and other reports
- Admission register
- Cumulative record
- Class attendance and leave record
- Clinical and field experience and students rotation

- Internal assessment register
- Mark list
- Record of extra curricular activities
- Practical record book
- Evaluation record

D. Staff Record

- Application forms
- Appointment orders
- Job description
- Periodic evaluation record
- Leave record
- Health record

E. Academic/ Administrative Record

- Philosophy / purpose of curriculum (Is the sum total of student activities that the school sponsors for the purpose of achieving its objectives)
- Course content/course plan
- Record of academic requirement
- Rotation plan
- Record of committees
- Stock record
- Affiliation record
- Annual reports
- Written policies
- Budget record
- Inspection/accreditation record (Is a process whereby any agency recognizes a college or school programme of study as having met certain predetermined standards.
- Minutes of meeting

Q 4. Care of records

=

Records:

- Records is a clinical, scientific, administrative legal document relating to the nursing care given to individual family and community.

Records are kept under safe custody of nurse in each ward.

- No individual sheet is separated from the complete record.
- Records are kept in place, which is not accessible to the patient and family members.
- No stranger is allowed to read records.
- Records are not handed over to legal advisors without written permission of administration.
- All health team members are legally and ethically obliged to keep in confidence all the information provided in records.
- All records are handed over carefully.
- All records has to be arranged according to the hospital rule. It can be arranged alphabetically, numerically, geographically.
- Records are never send out of the hospital/organization without the permission of concerned authority

Q 5. Principles of record writing

=

Records:

- Records is a clinical, scientific, administrative legal document relating to the nursing care given to individual family and community.
-

Records:

- Records is a clinical, scientific, administrative legal document relating to the nursing care given to individual family and community.
- As records serve as legal document, they should be written clearly , accurately, appropriately and legibly.
- All entries should be signed by the individual who writes them.
- Care to be taken not to make any errors on the records. If anything is crossed out, it should be dated and initiated.
- Records should be written in chronological order.
- Records should be written continuously without blank pages.
- Lengthy corrections of records are written as amendments.
- Each page of the records should be properly identified with the name, age, ward, date etc...
- Use only standard abbreviations,
- Records should be truthful , brief and complete,

CHAPTER SEVEN

UNIT 7: VITAL SIGNS

SHORT ANSWER QUESTION

Q 1. Factors affecting body temperature

= **Factors affecting body temperature**

1. Age- Infant- 0.5°C more than normal due to irregular activity, brown fat, premature thermoregulatory mechanism. Old age- subnormal temperature due to decrease activity, low BMR, weak thermoregulatory mechanism.

2. Sex- Females body temperature is slightly low due to low BMR, more subcutaneous fat. Temperature increases 0.5°C at the time of ovulation (Progesterone effects)

3. Diurnal variation- its up to 1.5°C. Lowest in early morning and maximum in evening.

4. Diseases- Increased in hyperthyroidism, malignancy. Decreased in hypothyroidism.

5. Exercise- It can cause increase up to 40-41°C / 104-106°F (inability of heat dissipating mechanism to handle that increased amount of heat). The body's rate of heat production can vary from ~70 kcal/hr at rest to 600 kcal/hr during jogging.

6. Emotional factor- Can increase approx. 2°C due to unconscious tensing of the muscle.

Q 2. STATES OF RIGOR

= **DEFINITION OF RIGOR** A rigor is a sever attack of shivering which may occur at the onset of disease characterised by a rise in temperature.

STATES OF RIGOR First stage- also called as cold stage.Patient shivers uncontrollably skin is cold. Face is pinched and pale,pluse is feeble and rapid. Temperature rises rapidly to 103 degree f. Patient will feel cold.

SECOND STAGE OF RIGOR It is also called as hot stage. During this stage patient become uncomfortably hot.His skin is very hot and dry. Patient will complain of extreme thirst and headache.Shivering stops.

THIRD STAGE OF RIGOR It is also called sweating stage. Patient begins to sweat profusely, temperature decreases,pluse rate also decreases.Discomfort subsides, patient may go into a state of shock and collapse, if not cared properly.

CARE OF PATIENT WITH RIGOR A patient suffering from rigor should never be left alone. First stage care- during shivering attack he should be given hot drinks and have blanket put around him,until he feels warm. Apply warmth with hot water bag.

CARE OF PATIENT WITH RIGOR SECOND STAGE CARE-during the hot stage patient should be given cool drinks, and cold compresses or an ice bag, applied to his head will help to relieve headaches. patient temperature is recorded every 10 to 15 min. Give tepid sponging. it is important to observe carefully for first signs of swatting. Remove all blankets and hot appliances .Cover patient with thin bed sheet.

CARE OF PATIENT WITH RIGOR THIRD STAGE CARE-Swating is one of the bodys usual ways of reducing temperature, but the swating must be wiped from pt's face, neck and chest. At the end of the rigor patient may feel very exhausted and nurse should ensure that the patient is comfortable.

CARE OF PATIENT WITH RIGOR Change patient's clothing and also change linen. Observation must be continued at regular intervals until the temperature has remained regular. Sweet drinks may be given to trat fatige. When temperature comes down and pluse is not improved it is considered as false crisis,and patient's condition may deteriorate.

Q 3. NURSING CARE OF PATIENT WITH PYREXIA / fever

= NURSING CARE OF PATIENT WITH PYREXIA NURSING INTERVENTION OF FEVER-

Maximize heat loss- Administation of cool drinks Application of cold compress and ice bags Cold sponging and cold packs. Cold bath Use of hypothermic blanket

NURSING CARE OF PATIENT WITH PYREXIA Prevent shivering-shivering is prevented because it increases metabolic activity Produces heat, increases oxygen demand, and circulation . May cause hyperventilation and respiratory alkalosis.

Promote client comfort- Encourage oral hygiene, Prevent dehydration Control temperature of environment. Provide complete bed rest The clothing should be light,loose, smooth, cotton,non irritating.

Satisty supplement for increased metabolic rate- provide supplemental oxygen therapy . Replace fluid lost Provide high caloric diet- because oxygen consumtion in body tissues increases. Diet should be easily digestible and palatable Fluid intake upto3000ml.

Encourage patient to take plenty of fluid. Maintain intake out put chart.Provide small frequent feeds.Make food palatable.Plenty of fluid and fruits will help to evacuate bowel regularly.

Maintenance of personal hygiene— Frequent mouth care Care of skin and pressure points. Give sponge bath daily.If temperature remains high cold sponging is given to bring down the temperature.

Safety of patient— Never leave a patient alone.Rigor and convulsions may occur at any time constant observation is important . Evaluate urine output periodically.

Q 4. Types of fever .

= **Defination :** Fever, also known as pyrexia and febrile response, is defined as having a temperature and also causing body to over heat due to an increase in the body's temperature set- point. There is not a single agreed upon upper limit for normal temperature with sources using values between 37.5 and 38.3 °C (99.5 and 100.9 °F),

TYPES OF FEVER

The pattern of temperature changes may occasionally hint at the diagnosis:

• **Continuous fever**: Temperature remains above normal throughout the day and does not fluctuate more than 1 °C in 24 hours, e.g. lobar pneumonia, typhoid, meningitis, urinary tract infection, brucellosis, or typhus. Typhoid fever may show a specific fever pattern (Wunderlich curve of typhoid fever), with a slow stepwise increase and a high plateau. (Drops due to fever-reducing drugs are excluded.)

• **Intermittent fever:** The temperature elevation is present only for a certain period, later cycling back to normal, e.g. malaria, kala-azar, pyaemia, or septicemia. Following are its types

• **Quotidian fever,** with a periodicity of 24 hours, typical of Plasmodium falciparum or Plasmodium knowlesi malaria

• **Tertian fever (**48-hour periodicity), typical of Plasmodium vivax or Plasmodium ovale malaria

• Quartan fever (72-hour periodicity), typical of Plasmodium malariae malaria.

Remittent fever: Temperature remains above normal throughout the day and fluctuates more than 1 °C in 24 hours, e.g., infective endocarditis.

• **Pel-Ebstein fever:** A specific kind of fever associated with Hodgkin's lymphoma, being high for one week and low for the next week and so on. However, there is some debate as to whether this pattern truly exists.

• **A neutropenic fever**: also called febrile neutropenia, is a fever in the absence of normal immune system function. Because of the lack of infection-fighting neutrophils, a bacterial infection can spread rapidly; this fever is, therefore, usually considered to require urgent medical attention. This kind of fever is more commonly seen in people receiving immune-suppressing chemotherapy than in apparently healthy people.

• **Febricula** is an old term for a low-grade fever, especially if the cause is unknown, no other symptoms are present, and the patient recovers fully in less than a week.

CHAPTER EIGHT

UNIT 8: HEALTH ASSESSMENT

- *SHORT ANSWER QUESTION*

Q 1. Purposes of health assessment

= **Health assessment:** It is a detailed study of the entire body in order to determine the general or mental condition of body

- To collect data about physical, mental and social well-being of client.
- To identify the problem in early stage.
- To determine the cause and extent of disease.
- To evaluate/monitor the changes in client's health status (deterioration or improvement).
- To determine the nature of treatment required for client.
- To alleviate the complications.
- To certify whether client is medically fit to resume duties.
- To collect data systematically.
- To identify client's strength, weakness, knowledge, motivation, support system and coping abilities.
- To compare the client's state of health with ideal state. Considering his age, gender, culture, physical, psychological and socio-economic status.

Q 2. Methods of physical examination

= METHODS OF EXAMINING

Four primary techniques are used in the physical examination:

1. Inspection

- Inspection is the deliberate, purposeful, and systematic visual examination of the body which involves careful and keen observation of the client's general appearance, body size, shape, stature, gait & posture.
- It begins as soon as nurse interacts with client.
- The nurse inspects with the naked eye and with a lighted instrument such as an otoscope
- It involves;
- Inspection involves visualize the body area to maximum extent then compare it with other side of body. E.g. compare the width of left arm with right arm.
- Sufficient exposure of body area is very important.
- Observe colour, texture, mobility, symmetry, nutritional status.
- General appearance : & State of consciousness
- Expression; Anxious, Comfortable, Alert, Nervous
- Body build: Thin / Fatty / Moderate
- **2. PALPATION:**Is the use of tactile sensation (use of touch, hands, fingers) to feel texture, size, shape, consistency and placement/location of organs.
- The pads of the fingers are used because their concentration of nerve endings makes them highly sensitive to tactile discrimination.
- Gentle touch used to detect characteristics of skin and superficial tissues.
- Gentle/ Light palpation is attained by pressing 1cm in depth for assessing skin, pulse palpation and tenderness.
- Deep palpation involves use of both hands to press 4 cm in depth to determine organ size and contour deep palpation is done to examine deep organs (liver) and to relive pain.
- **General guidelines for palpation**

- Deep palpation using the lower hand to support the body while the upper hand palpates the organ.
- The nurse's hands should be clean and warm, and the fingernails short.
- Areas of tenderness should be palpated last.
- Deep palpation should be done after superficial palpation.
- Gowning and/or draping the client appropriately.
- Positioning the client comfortably.

3. Percussion

Percussion is the act of striking the body surface to elicit sounds that can be heard or vibrations that can be felt.

Types of percussion:

i. Direct percussion

- The nurse strikes the area to be percussed directly with the pads of two, three, or four fingers or with the pad of the middle finger.
- The strikes are rapid, and the movement is from the wrist
- This technique is not generally used to percuss the thorax but is useful in percussing an adult's sinuses.

ii. Indirect percussion

- Is the striking of an object (e.g., a finger) held against the body area to be examined.
- In this technique, the middle finger of the non dominant hand, referred to as the pleximeter, is placed firmly on the client's skin.
- Only the distal phalanx and joint of this finger should be in contact with the skin.
- Using the tip of the flexed middle finger of the other hand, called the plexor, the nurse strikes the pleximeter, usually at the distal interphalangeal joint
- Some may find a point between the distal and proximal joints to be a more comfortable pleximeter point.

- The motion comes from the wrist; the forearm remains stationary.
- The angle between the plexor and the pleximeter should be 90 degrees, and the blows must be firm, rapid, and short to obtain a clear sound.
- Percussion is used to determine the size and shape of internal organs by establishing their borders.
- It indicates whether tissue is fluid filled, air filled, or solid.

Percussion elicits five types of sound:

1. Tympany (normal) heard over abdomen.
2. Resonance normal lung tissue.
3. Hyper resonance over inflated lungs.
4. Dullness over lungs
5. Flatness over muscle.

4.Auscultation

- It is the process of listening to sounds produced within the body.
- Auscultation may be direct or indirect.
- Directauscultation is the use of the unaided ear. E.g.;to listen to a respiratory wheeze.
- Indirectauscultation is the use of a stethoscope, which transmits the sounds to the nurse's ears. A stethoscope is used primarily to listen to sounds from within the body such as bowel sounds or valve sounds of the heart and blood pressure.

The stethoscope;

- Tubing of it should be 30 to 35 cm long, with an internal diameter of about 0.3 cm (1/8 in.).
- It should have both a flat disc diaphragm and a bell-shaped amplifier

- The diaphragm best transmits high-pitched sounds (e.g., bronchial sounds),
- And the bell best transmits low-pitched sounds such as some heart sounds. The earpieces of the stethoscope should fit comfortably into the nurse's ears, facing forward.
- The amplifier of the stethoscope is placed firmly but lightly against the client's skin.

Q 3. What is physical examination

= Defination ;

Health assessment is systemic assement of human body Which involves the use of human body which involves the use of one's senses to determine the general physical and mental conditions of the body.

Physical examination is defined as a complete assessment of a patient's physical and mental status.

A physical examination is a systemic collection of objective information that is directly observed or is elicited through examination techniques.

CHAPTER NINE

UNIT 9: MACHINERY, EQUIPMENT AND LINEN

SHORT ANSWER QUESTION

Q 1 Care of linen

= Linen is a fabric made from fibres of flax plant. It includes clothes, sheets etc. In hospital setting, linens are used for many purposes: covering the bed, client, articles etc.

- **List of linen used in hospital setting**
- Bed sheets : bottom and top, draw sheets, pack sheet
- Blankets
- Curtains
- Cloth covers: Pillows, mattress, hot water bottle, ice collar, ice cap, air cushion, inhaler cover, and sand bag cover.
- Towels : Bath, hand, dressing, doctor's towel
- Wrappers for tray, dressing set, gloves, syringes.
- Client's clothes: Shirt, pajama, gown, leggings.
- Staff's clothes: Mask, cap, gown, shirt, pajama.
- Binders, Bandages
- Restraints - Elbow
- Dusters, mittens
- Others: Diet napkins, tray covers
- **Importance of maintaining linen in hospital**
- Clean and tidy bed gives an aesthetic sense to the client as well as to hospital employee.

- It enhances comfort of client
- It limits the cross-infection, infestation with bugs.
- It promotes cost - effectiveness of hospital by prolonging the life of these items.
- **Cleaning and care of linen:**
- Follow hospital policy for maintenance of Linen.
- Store the clean and unused Linen in cupboard and maintain stock register.
- Fold and keep different linen sorted out in cupboard.
- Send indent timely to keep extra linen at hand.
- Always maintain laundry record register.
- Regularly inspect and send torn linen for repair to prevent further damage.
- Regularly send the dirty linen to laundry for washing and ironing.
- Dust the mattress with dry/damp cloth.
- Bed sheets can be protected from stains soils by drawing mackintosh.
- Always use mackintosh over top linen while doing any therapeutic or diagnostic procedure.
- Try to clean the fresh stains immediately with solvent.
- Teach the importance of keeping clean hospital linen to the client, family members.
- **Contaminated Linen**
- Always use laundry box/hamper trolley for putting contaminated linen, should not be put on floor as it will cause more contamination.
- Dip the linen in a bucket containing 0.5% solution of chlorine for 10 minutes. Make sure Bucket is covered with lid otherwise chlorine gas will evaporate.
- Rinse it in water and get dry in sun.
- Send for autoclaving.
- Many hospitals have practice of cleaning linen with strong detergents.

- After disinfecting the linen, store them in appropriate cupboards.
- **General Instructions To Remove Stain**
- Note the color and the material stained
- Try the simplest method.
- Remove stain as soon as possible.
- Try with cold water first.
- For colored material always try the remover on a small part.
- If the stain contains fat materials hot water and soap to be used.
- When the stains do not respond to simple methods bleaching agents such as lemon juice, hydrogen peroxide and bleaching powder can be used.
- When using boiling water for removal, stretch the stained part over a bowl and pour the boiling water in force until the stain disappears.
- When using acid for removal, stretch the stained part over a bowl of boiling water and apply acid by means of medicine dropper
- When bleaching by sunlight wet the stained area and lay it in the sunlight.
- **Blanket:**
- As frequent washing of Blanket is irksome work, it must be dusted in open place then dry heat (sunlight) is given for 15-20 minutes.
- **Pillow-Mattresses:**
- Disinfect by keeping in sunlight for 15-20 minutes.
- In case of any stain, bloody soil, keep that area in chlorine bleach.
- Avoid excessive folding of mattress as it may cause its breakage.
- Extra - pillow and mattress should be stored in separate room by placing them on long flat surface.
- Naphthalene balls can be placed in between the layer to protect from moths and mites.

Q 2 Care of rubber goods

= Equipments or articles made up of rubber come under this category. List of rubber articles commonly used in hospital is as follows

- Mackintosh
- Rubber tubing's - rectal, flatus, catheter, gavage, and lavage.
- Gloves (Reusable)
- Mouthpiece of AMBU bag
- Bulb used with asepto syringe and breast pump.
- Hot water bottle, air pillow, ice caps, air cushion etc.
- Suction tubing's
- **Points to remember while doing care of rubber Items:**
- Avoid use of kerosene, benzene, oils, heat for cleaning rubber item. (Rubber has quality to expand or contract, thus leading to damage).
- Rubber sheets are folded by rolling them to avoid breakage.
- Avoid using sharp articles like blade, pins as they can cut rubber easily.
- Store rubber items in wooden cupboards not in metallic ones because metal is more sensitive to temperature than wood.
- Dry the rubber items in shade
- **CLEANING OF RUBBER MACKINTOSH**
- Spread the mackintosh on a table or a flat surface and wet it with cold water
- Rub the upper surface with soap and water using a clean cloth or towel
- Turn the other side and repeat the process as above
- Wash both surfaces under running water
- If stains are present care should be taken to remove them by appropriate methods
- For disinfection, use Lysol or dettol 1:40
- Hang them on a horizontal cylindrical pole in shade to dry. Spread them without wrinkles
- When both surfaces are absolutely dry, powder them lightly with French chalk powder

- Store them either flat or rolled and never fold, taking care to see that two mackintosh surfaces do not lie together but are separated by old linen or paper.
- **CARE OF RUBBER GLOVES**
- It is desired that the wearer of the gloves should wash them on their hands just before they are removed to prevent adherence of blood and other organic materials
- After removing from the hands they are washed with soap and cold water, first on the outside, then invert and repeat on the inside
- Rinse well with water both inside and outside as described above
- Holes and tears are discovered by submerging the glove filled with air in the water. If there are holes the bubbles will pass up through the water. Separate torn gloves.
- **CARE OF THE RUBBER TUBES**
- (catheters, rectal tubes, flatus tube, ryles tube, and infusion sets)
- The points to remember in cleaning of the tubes are:
- After use wash them under running water holding the eye end upwards and allowing the water to run through
- A small quantity of organic matter may be lodged at the eye end. Remove them using a swab stick
- Clean them with soap and warm water to remove the dirt and grease
- Wash them again under running water
- Boil the tubes for 5min by putting them in the boiling water. Dry them by hanging
- When dried, powder and store them in airtight containers lengthwise
- Reboil or autoclave them before use
- **CLEANING OF THE AIR CUSHION, RUBBER BEDS, HOT WATER BOTTLES, ICE CAPS, AND ICE COLLARS**
- To clean the air cushion and airbeds do not pour water into them. It is sufficient to clean the outside.

- During cleaning it should not filled with air because while rubbing there is tendency to exert pressure and they may crack or weaken.
- The valves of the air cushions or beds should never be immersed in water as it spoils them
- Cleaning and storing are done like other rubber goods except that they should be slightly inflated to prevent the two surfaces to come in contact with each **other.**
- **In case of hot water bottles, ice caps and ice collars, empty the contents immediately after use.**
- **Wash and dry as in the case of other rubber goods**
- **Hang the bags upside down to drain the water**
- **The ice bags which cannot be hung are dried with a piece of cloth**
- **When the bags are completely dried inflate them with air**
- **The covers of the air cushion, ice bags and ice collars are disinfected and sent to the laundry for washing**
- **Ambubag with mouth piece**
- Clean the rubber part with a clean cloth,
- Disinfect it using methylated spirit swab.
- Clean it the same way as ambubag cleaned.
- **Bulb of syringe**
- After cleaning, apply little powder on bulb and store it in dry and cool place.
-

CHAPTER TEN

UNIT 10: MEETING NEEDS OF PATIENT

SHORT ANSWER QUESTION

Q 1. Basic human needs

= **BASIC NEEDS OR ACTIVITIES OF DAILY LIVING (ADL)**

Activities of daily livings are the activities usually performed in the course of a normal day in

the individual's life such as eating, working or brushing the teeth.

ACTIVITIES OF ADL INCLUDES

1. **Maintaining safe environment**: To achieve personal & domestic cleanliness & aimed at

decreasing the number of microorganisms to maintain a safe environment.

2. Communication: Communication is the process of exchanging thoughts, ideas, of

feeling from one individual to others. ? Verbal &nonverbal communication

3. Breathing: In the breathing process, the cell of the body receives air,(oxygen) essential

for all the body cells , without which human life will not exist.

4. Eating & drinking: They are essential activities of the daily living. Human life cannot

be sustained for all the body cells, without eating & drinking. Many people in the world

die daily due to starvation.

5. Eliminating: Eliminating (bath, urinary &faecal) likes eating & drinking is necessary &

on integral activity of everyday life, eliminating is regard as a highly private activity.

6.Personal cleansing &Dressing: Activities included are washing, bathing, care of hair,

nails, teeth, mouth & clothing.

7. Controlling body temperature: Regulation of body temperature is essential for

different biological processes. People have to avoid the hazards & discomfort of heat &

cold by varying the amount of clothing , regulating the amount of physical activity, etc

8. Mobilizing: Mobilizing includes the movement produced by groups of large muscles

(e.g. facial expression &gestures).

9. Working &Playing: Work & play are important for physical & mental health.

10. Sleeping: Essential for healthy living, the body process does not stop during sleep. All

individual have periods of activity & sleep.

Q 2. Maslow's hierarchy of needs

= MASLAW'S HIERARCHY OF NEEDS

Abraham Maslow developed a hierarchy of human needs. In this theory, he stated that

individuals must satisfy lower level deficit needs before progressing to meet higher-level growth

needs.

This hierarchy of human needs arranged the basic human needs in five level of priority as follows;

1. Physiological needs

2. Safety and security needs

3. Love and belonging needs

4. Self-esteem needs

5. Self-actualization needs

1. Physiological needs- according to Maslow, these needs are located at the base of the hierarchy of needs, which are very essential to life therefore; they are placed in top priority when unsatisfied and remain as having highest priority until satisfied.

They are basic needs which include air (oxygen), water (fluid), food (nutrition), clothing (to maintain temperature), shelter (comfortable room), elimination, sexuality, physical activity and rest. Physiological needs are essential needs for survival.

Oxygen- it is most essential of all the needs; all body cells require oxygen for survival. Nurses evaluate oxygen by assessing skin color, vital signs.

Physical activity and rest- these are also basic physiological needs. These activities are accomplished by intact functioning of muscular and body system. The area of nursing responsibilities in these needs are to maintain nutrition, providing sleep and rest, support elimination process, prevention of complication, assurance of physiological status and health maintenance.

2. Safety and security needs Physical safety-it means protecting a person from potential or actual harm.

Areas of nursing responsibility included in physical safety are providing comfort, insisting physical exercise, i.e. Precautions, maintaining personal hygiene. Providing or creating safety environment, etc. Nurses carry out variety of activities to meet clients' physical safety. These activities are as follows:

Hand washing and using sterile technique to prevent infection.

Using electrical equipment properly with precautions.

Administering medications knowledgeably.

Using skill moving and ambulating patients.

Emotional safety- it involves trusting others and being free from fear, anxiety, and apprehension.

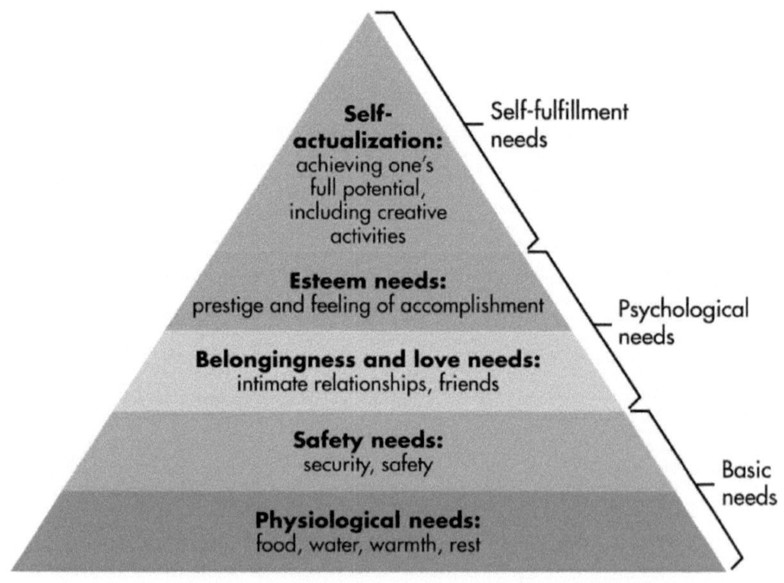

MASLAW'S HIERARCHY OF NEEDS

3. Love and belonging needs

After physiological and safety needs have been fulfilled, the third level of human needs is social and involves feelings of belongingness. The need for interpersonal relationships motivates behaviour. Love and belonging are the needs or social affiliation, in which person expects

meaningful interpersonal relationship, group acceptance, and love and belonging.

Examples include friendship, intimacy, trust, and acceptance, receiving and giving affection and

love. Affiliating, being part of a group (family, friends, work).

4.Esteem needs - Maslow classified esteemed need into two categories: (i) esteem for oneself

(dignity, achievement, mastery, and independence) and (ii) the desire for reputation or respect

from others (e.g., status, prestige).

Maslow indicated that the need for respect or reputation is most important for children and

adolescents and precedes real self-esteem or dignity.

5. Self-actualization needs - Realizing personal potential, self-fulfilment, seeking personal

growth and peak experiences. A desire "to become everything one is capable of becoming."

Implication of human need in nursing

Knowledge of human needs helps nurses to:

1. Understand them, so that they can meet their personal needs outside the health care setting,

e.g. maintenance of body temperature.

2. Set priorities as in giving care. e.g., Working & playing will assume a low priority during a

period of critical illness.

3. Better to understand patient's behavior so that they can respond therapeutically rather than

emotionally e.g. a patient putting on his signal light repeatedly may convey the message of need

for safety.

4. Relieve the distress of patient's e.g. helping a patient to meet his unmet need of love &

affection.

Q 3. Role of nurse in providing safe and clean environment

= **Role of nurse in providing safe and clean environment**

This is the duty of the health care staff to ensure an ideal atmosphere for patient, recovery or

relaxation. Noise, temperature and light levels are all essential, but environmental cleanliness is

critical, maintaining a sensation of health and comfort and fostering a sense of safety and

comfort and promoting an atmosphere of competent caring.

The role of nurse in providing safe and clean environment-

1.Ensure units are well ventilated

2.Ensure noise is within the normal level

3.Ensure optimum temperature of the ward

4. Ensure rodent/pest control

5. Provide sufficient light

6.Update safety precautions for fire

Q 4. Strokes used in back massage

= Different techniques of back massage

1 Effleurage (gliding or stroking) - it means a long soothing, stroking movement which are performed using palm to the hand or fingers. Apply oil evenly to the entire body. Relax the hands and mould them towards the contours of the body.

- Effleurage is used at the start of a massage; it helps in soothing and helping the patient get used to relax.

2. Petrissage (kneading or milking)- the movements which involve various ways of kneading, rolling and picking up the skin and muscles, is called petrissage. It is performed by starting first with the fingers pointing away from nurse, then pressing down with the palm, grasping the flesh between finger and thumb and pushing it towards the other hand. A continuous action is followed which involves alternating the hands to squeeze and release.

- Petrissage attempts to increase circulation with clearing out toxins from muscle and nerve tissue.

3.Friction- Use small circular strokes using thumb along the sides of spinal column and place rest of the fingers on the side of thumb and move forward from sacral vertebra to cervical vertebral column in a synchronized manner. Using the thumb, fingertips or knuckles,· one can apply the deep direct pressure to one particular site. Press few second then gradually release.· Remember not to do on top of the spinal cord.

- Assists in realigning scar tissue, relaxes muscle by stimulating tendon reflex.

4. hacking or Vibration or shaking or jostling Moving the hand back and forth on the client's body without leaving contact a continuous trembling, pressing movement made with the hands or fingers.

-It boosts circulation and increases the power of the muscle to contact.

5.taping or tapeotment The fast and stimulating movements of massage are termed as tapeotment,or percussion movement. This includes cupping and pounding. The speed and rhythm of the movement will be brisk and firm, alternating the hands, without too much thumping.

-These movements stimulate the blood circulation, tone and help strengthen sagging skin muscles, especially the soft tissue areas, such as thighs and buttocks, which are prone to cellulite

Q 5. Steps of back massage

= Steps Of Procedure ;

1.Perform hand hygiene

2 Assemble all equipments required.

3 Check the client's identification and condition

4 Explain to the client about the purpose and the Procedure.

5 Put all required equipments to the bed-side and Set up.

6 close all windows and doors, and put the screen Or / and utilize the curtain if there is

7. placing the appropriate position: 1) Move the client near towards you. 2) turn the client to her/his side and put the mackintosh covered by big towel under the client's body.

8 Expose the client's back fully and observe it Whether if there are any abnormalities.

9. Lather soap by sponge towel. Wipe with soap and Rinse with plain warm water.

10 Put some lotion or oil into your palm. Apply the Oil or the lotion and massage at least 3-5Minutes by placing the palms: 1) from sacral region to neck 2)from upper shoulder to the lowest parts of Buttocks

Different techniques of back massage

1. **Effleurage (gliding or stroking)** - it means a long soothing, stroking movement which are performed using palm to the hand or fingers. Apply oil evenly to the entire body. Relax the hands and mould them towards the contours of the body.

- Effleurage is used at the start of a massage; it helps in soothing and helping the patient get used to relax.

2. Petrissage (kneading or milking)- the movements which involve various ways of kneading, rolling and picking up the skin and muscles, is called petrissage. It is performed by starting first with the fingers pointing away from nurse, then pressing down with the palm, grasping the flesh between finger and thumb and pushing it towards the other hand. A continuous action is followed which involves alternating the hands to squeeze and release.

- Petrissage attempts to increase circulation with clearing out toxins from muscle and nerve tissue.

3.Friction- Use small circular strokes using thumb along the sides of spinal column and place rest of the fingers on the side of thumb and move forward from sacral vertebra to cervical vertebral column in a synchronized manner. Using the thumb, fingertips or knuckles,· one can apply the deep direct pressure to one particular site. Press few second then gradually release.· Remember not to do on top of the spinal cord.

- Assists in realigning scar tissue, relaxes muscle by stimulating tendon reflex.

4. hacking or Vibration or shaking or jostling Moving the hand back and forth on the client's body without leaving contact a continuous trembling, pressing movement made with the hands or fingers.

-It boosts circulation and increases the power of the muscle to contact.

5.taping or tapeotment The fast and stimulating movements of massage are termed as tapeotment,or percussion movement. This includes cupping and pounding. The speed and rhythm of the movement will be brisk and firm, alternating the hands, without too much thumping.

-These movements stimulate the blood circulation, tone and help strengthen sagging skin muscles, especially the soft tissue areas, such as thighs and buttocks, which are prone to cellulite

Q 6. Safety devices

= **SAFETY DEVICES**

A safety device is a piece of equipment that reduces loss or damage from an accident, or breakin.

Safety devices are

1. Restraints

2. Side rails

3. Trapeze

4. Wheel chair with belt

5. Stretcher with belt

6. Fixed and strong bed

7. Identification band /wrist band

1. Restraints: Restraints are used to restrict the movements of the sick patient in the bed.

Definition- A restraint is any manual method that immobilizes or reduces the ability of a

patient to move his/her arms, legs, body or head freely.

Purposes of restraints

To keep a person in proper position and prevent movement or from falling.

To control or prevent harmful behaviour. patients need restraints so that they should not interrupt the therapy. Scratch their skin

b. Remove catheters and tubes that give them medicine and fluids

c. Get out of bed, fall, and hurt themselves

d. Harm other people

General Instructions of using restraints.

1. Explain the need for application and type of restraints.

2. Need should be made to understand the family and friends of the client

3. Restraints should be used with great care.

4. Assistance should be taken.

5. Allow freedom to move.

6. Circulation must not be occluded by restraints.

7. Pad the bony prominences.

8. While applying restraints, see that the normal body positions can be assumed.

9. Untie the restraints every 4 hours.

10. Client with restraints should be visited atleast every 30-60 minutes.

11. Do not apply linen restraints with a regular knot.

12. Fasten restraint to bed frame and not to side-rails.

13. Never use restraints over an IV site.

14. While removing, remove one restraint at a time.

15. Skin folds should be clean and dry prior to application of restrain.

16. Ensure that there are no wrinkles in restraint.

2. Side rails: Side rails are attached to both sides of the bed to prevent the client from getting

out or falling out of the bed.

Objectives

1. To prevent the client from getting out of bed.

2. To prevent the client from falling out of bed.

3. To observe the client.

4. To prevent the type of injury.

Uses of side rails

1. Client with altered level of consciousness,

2. The elderly clients.
3. The debilitated clients.
4. Children

3. Trapeze

A trapeze, a horizontal bar hanging on chains, is often attached to a large overhead frame, which itself attaches to the bed .The trapeze is used by the client to pull up to a sitting position or to lift the shoulders and hips off the bed.

4. Wheel chair with belt

Benefits- • helps to transfer the patient.

Figure: Bed with side rails

• provides proper fit & postural support.
• It is safe and durable.
• It meets the patients' needs and environmental conditions.
• To protect the patient from fall.

5. Stretcher with belt

Benefits • To ensure safety of the patient.
• making patient care safer.
• To transfer the patient.

6. Fixed and strong bed

Benefits • better positioning for patients
• improved circulation
• promote patient safety
• Aid to transfer the patient.
• To give sound sleep.

7. Identification band /wrist band

Benefits • identify the patient correctly.
• To deliver quality care in a safe environment.
• Patient information can easily be read by staff.

Q 7. Purpose of Comfort devices And Types of comfort devices

= COMFORT DEVICES

Comfort - Comfort is a state of free from pain and discomfort tension and anxiety.

Comfort is defined as the contented enjoyment in physical or mental wellbeing freedom from

pain or trouble.

Meaning of comfort- comfort is a sense of mental and physical wellbeing. Physical comfort gets

affected due to a dirty and wet bed and lack of body alignment. High temperature and humidity,

poor ventilation, noise, unpleasant odour and glaring light make the patient uncomfortable.

Comfort devices are invented article which would add to the comfort of the patient when used in

the appropriate manner, by relieving the discomfort and helping to maintain correct posture.

Purpose of comfort devices

1. To promote comfort.

2. To prevent discomfort.

3. To alleviate discomfort.

4. To ensure that the patient has rest.

5. To assist the patient to obtain an adequate sleep to meet his requirement.

6. To maintain correct posture.

1 Pillow: Used for support to maintain correct body

alignment.

Purpose

To relieve dyspnoea.

To promote drainage from abdominal cavity.

To provide a comfortable change of position.

2 Backrest : It is a mechanical device which provides support for the patient in sitting position

3. Bed cradle : It is a frame used to hold the bed linen from touching the patient.

4. Cardiac table:

Usually for patient who are propped up in a

sitting position for change of position. Bed

table placed in front with a pillow on it,

patient can lean forward & take rest table
without pillow is used for writing & meals
used for possible to use accessory muscle of
respiration position should be changed to
relieve fatigue & prevent embolism.

5. Knee rest:

Knee rest may be substituted by a pillow, gives relaxation and thus
relieves pain on abdominal muscle and tendons beneath the knees.

6. Trapeze bar:

Trapeze bar is suspended from an overhead frame that
extends from the foot to head of bed patient can grasp
the bar to raise the trunk off the bed surface or to
move up in bed.

7. Fracturedboard:

It is a support that is placed under patient mattress to give added rigidity
to the mattress. Usually made of wood/canvas& is constructed to fit the
standard hospital bed.

8. Foot rest:

Foot board is the device that is placed towards the foot of patient's bed to
serve as support for his feet some fit onto the sides of bed frame & rest on
the mattress at any point along the bed usually made of
wood/plastic/heavy canvas.

9. Bradfordframe:

It is a canvas stretcher like device that is supported by blocks on the
foundation of bed. Used to immobilize patient who have injured spines.

Canvas is divided into parts so that small centre portion can be removed to insert a bedpan.

10. Trochanterboard:

Trochanter rolls prevents external rotation of legs when patient is in supine position. A cotton bath blanket sheet is folded lengthwise to width extending from greater trochanter of femur to lower boarder of popliteal space. Blanket is placed under the buttocks rolled away from the patient until thigh is in neutral position with patella facing upward bradford frame.

11. Sand bags:

Provide support & shape to body contours immobilize extremities & maintain specific body alignment. They are filled plastic bags that can be shaped to body contours can be used in place of or in addition to trochanter rolls.

12. Hand rolls:

Hand rolls maintain thumb in slightly adducted in opposition to fingers in slightly flexed position can be made by folding a washcloth in half, rolling in lengthwise & securing roll with tape. Roll is placed against palmer surface of hand sand bags.

13. Hand wrist splints:

Individually melded for the patient to maintain proper alignment of the thumb in slight adduction and wrist in slight dorsiflexion. These splints should be used for the patient whom the splint was made.

14. Air and water mattress :

These are used for very thin, obese and those who are prone to bedsore.

The principle exerted on the bony prominences will be equally distributed

in all direction. Thus pressure against bony prominences or areas subject

to develop pressure sores will be reduced.

15. Rubber & cotton rings :

It is used to relieve pressure on certain parts of the body like elbows and heels.

16. Air cushions :

It is used to take off the weight of the body and to relieve pressure on

certain parts of the body like elbows and heels.

17. Bed blocks:

These are made of wood, may be high or low. These are placed under the foot of the bed for various reasons.

18. Thigh roll :

These are made by folding a sheet to a desired length of 23 feet and then rolled into a tight cylinder. These are used to support the hips and thighs, preventing them outward rotation and keeping the feet in good alignment, in case of paralysis, fracture of the femur or hip surgery

Q 8. Causes of pressure sores

= Causes of pressure sores

a. Direct or immediate cause- the pressure is caused by the weight of the body continuously

remaining in one position, splints, casts and bandages.

b. Friction- friction of the skin with rough bedding causes injury to the skin. The friction is

caused by wrinkles in the bed cloths, cramps of food in the bed, chipped or rough bed pans

and hard surfaces of plaster casts and splints.

c. Moisture-the skin contact with moisture for a prolong period can lead maceration of the skin.

d. Pressure of pathogenic organisms- due to unhygienic condition pathogenic organic

multiplies and infection settles on the skin.

Predisposing factors

1. Patient with long term illness, fracture patients.
2. Patient with spinal injury
3. Paralysis and limited movements
4. Emaciated and malnourished patients
5. Elderly and circulatory problems
6. Obese patients
7. Oedematous patients
8. Patient with incontinence
9. Diabetic patients with ulcers (diabetic foot)

Q 9. Prevention of bed sores

= Bedsores — also called pressure ulcers and decubitus ulcers — are injuries to skin and underlying tissue resulting from prolonged pressure on the skin. Bedsores most often develop on skin that covers bony areas of the body, such as the heels, ankles, hips and tailbone

Preventive measures of bedsore

1. Identification of clients who are particularly prone to the development of decubitus ulcer.

2. Confirm the high risk patients and daily examination for the signs and symptoms.

3. Relieve pressure by using special mattress, beds and comfort devices.

4. Change position of the client every 2 hourly and give back care all bedridden patients.

5. Loosening tight bandages and restraints.

6. Avoid friction by providing smooth, firm and wrinkle free bed, keep the bottom clothes

free from crumbs and foreign bodies.

7. Keep the patient clean and dry. Prevent moisture by changing linen when, it is wet or

soiled.

8. Giving back care to patients immediately following micturition and defecation.

9. Avoid physical or mechanical injury to the skin from improper fitting of prosthesis or

from burns caused by excessively hot or cold applications.

10. Use a bed cradle to lift the weight of bed linen off the patient to enable him or her to

move in bed freely.

11. Supply well balanced diet and adequate fluids to maintain general health of the patient.

Q 10. Types of beds

= A hospital bed or hospital cot is a bed specially designed for hospitalized patients or others in need of some form of health care. These beds have special features both for the comfort and well-being of the patient and for the convenience of health care workers.

Types of bed-

1. Simple or admission bed
2. Open bed
3. Closed bed
4. Occupied bed
5. Cardiac bed
6. Renal bed or rheumatism bed
7. Operation bed
8. Fracture bed/divided bed/amputed bed/Burn bed

Types of bed according to the ward

MEDICAL BED

1. Admission bed
2. Open bed or simple occupied bed
3. Closed bed or unoccupied bed
4. Cardiac bed

5. Renal bed

Surgical Bed

1. Admission bed
2. Operation bed
3. Fracture bed
4. Amputation /divided bed

Q 11. Purposes of bed making

= **Definition:**

It is a process of making neat and clean bed for the client in hospital.

It is a technique of preparing different types of bed for the patients to provide comfort in

his/ her suitable position for a particular condition.

Bed making is a systemic way of preparing the appropriate bed based on the condition of

the patient, which adopts scientific principles of nursing.

Bed making is a process of keeping the bed clean, neat and tidy. Also keep ready for

admission, transfer, examination, treatment and to promote comfort for the patient.

Purpose:

- To provide clean and comfortable bed to the patient.
- To observe and prevent bed complications
- To keep the bed ready for any emergency.
- To receive the client comfortably.
- To save time, effort and material.
- To provide active and passive exercise to the client
- To provide a neat appearance of the unit or ward.
- To adapt the needs of the patient.
- To prevent bedsore
- To provide rest and sleep
- To provide cleanliness and security.
- To establish an effective nurse patient relationship in order to assess the nursing needs of

the patients.

Q 12. Purposes of cardiac bed

= Cardiac bed

A cardiac bed is used to help the client assume a sitting position which can afford him greatest

amount of comfort with least strain. The main purpose of cardiac bed is to relieve dyspnea

caused by cardiac disease.

Purpose

• To relieve dyspnea.

• To make the patient as comfortable as possible when sitting upright.

• To prevent complication.

• To assist recovery of the patient.

Q 13. Factors affecting sleep .

= Rest is defined as a state of relatively decreased bodily work, either physical, mental or both, which leaves the individual feeling refreshed and relieved

Sleep is a basic human need; it is a universal biological process common to all people. Humans spend about one-third of their lives asleep.

FACTORS AFFECTING SLEEP

- **Illness:** Illness that causes pain or physical distress (e.g. arthritis, back pain) can result in sleep problems.
- **Environment:** Can promote or hinder sleep. Any change for example noise in the environment- can inhibit sleep. The absence of usual stimuli or the presence of unfamiliar stimuli can prevent people from sleeping.
- **Lifestyle:** Following an irregular morning and night time schedule can affect sleep. Moderate exercise in the morning or early afternoon usually is conducive to sleep, but exercise late in the day can delay sleep. Night shift workers frequently obtain less sleep than other workers and have difficulty falling asleep after getting off work.

- **Emotional stress:** Stress is considered by most sleep experts to be the number one cause of short term sleeping difficulties. A person preoccupied with personal problems may be unable to relax sufficiently to get to sleep.
- **Stimulants and alcohol:** Caffeine containing beverages acts as stimulants of the central nervous system. People who drink an excessive amount of alcohol often find their sleep disturbed
- **Smoking:** Nicotine has a stimulating effect on the body and smokers often have more difficulty falling asleep than non smokers do
- **Motivation:** Can increase alertness in some situations (e.g. a tire person can probably stay alert while attending an interesting concert).
- **Medications:** Some medications affect the quality of sleep. Eg hypnotics, narcotics
- **Diet:**
- Weight loss has been associated with reduced total sleep time as well as broken sleep and earlier awakening. Weight gain, on the other hand, seems to be associated with an increase in total sleep time, less broken sleep and later waking.
- Dietary L-tryptophan found, for example in cheese and milk-may induce sleep, a fact that might explain why warm milk helps some people get to sleep.

Q 14. Factors affecting nutrition of patients .

= It is the sum total of all the interaction that occurs between an organism and the food it consumes.

- Maintenance of good nutrition implies adequate intake of food
- Sufficient in quantity and of good quality, which supply the body with all nutrients needed for growth, maintenance and physical activity.

FACTORS AFFECTING NUTRITION

- **Religion**: Religious practices affect the intake of food. For example some religion allow to take only vegetables and not animals.
- **Development:** People in rapid periods of growth (i.e. infancy and adolescence) have increased needs for nutrients. Older people on the other hand need fewer calories and dietary changes in view of the risk of coronary heart disease, osteoporosis and hypertension.
- **Gender:** Nutrient requirements are different for men and women because of body composition and reproductive functions. The larger muscle mass of men translates into a greater need for calories and proteins. Because of menstruation women require iron than men do prior to menopause. Pregnant and lactating women have increased caloric and fluid needs.
- **Ethnicity and culture:** Ethnicity often determines food preferences. Traditional foods (e.g. rice for Asians, pasta for Italians, and curry for Indians) are eaten long after other customs are abandoned. In Indian scenario traditional people does not allow pregnant women to take papaya, water melon etc.
- **Economic status:** What to eat, how much to eat and how frequently to eat is affected by the economic status of individual. For example taking meal three times a day is the wish of a poor man
- **Biological factors:** Such as illness, chemotherapy, intake of drugs also influences the appetite.
- **Personal preferences:** Interest, food habits, fasting habits, physique consciousness, beauty consciousness all are associated with food preferences.
- **Psychological factors:** Level of stress, emotions- appetite increases during happiness but diminishes with stress
- **Alcohol abuse:** Excessive intake of alcohol may lead to nutritional deficiencies in a number of ways. It may depress appetite
- **Environmental factors:** Such as temperature has great influence on food preference. During cold more energy is required so

people prefer to take dry fruits.

Q 15. Indication of nasogastric tube feeding

= **DEFINITION:** It is the insertion of a tube into the oesophagus and stomach through the nose.

- **INDICATIONS OF NASOGASTRIC FEEDING:**
- When the patient is unable to ingest, chew or swallow food but is still able to digest and absorb nutrient, a tube feeding is indicated. E.g. in case of unconscious and semi conscious patients etc.
- When the patient is too weak to swallow food or when the conditions makes it difficult to take a large amount of food orally e.g. Acute and chronic infections, severe burns, malnutrition and prematurity.
- When the patient is unable to retain foods, e.g. vomiting, anorexia nervosa etc.
- When the condition of the mouth or oesophagus makes swallowing difficult or impossible e.g. in case of post operative patients
- For a patient who refuses to take food e.g. patients with depression

Q 16. Methods of oxygen administration

= **Oxygenation:** Is the process that includes both the inspiratory and expiratory activities hence there occurs the exchange/ transport of respiratory gases.

METHODS OF OXYGEN ADMINISTRATION.

1.Cannula:

- The nasal cannula (nasal prongs) is the most common and inexpensive device used to administer oxygen.
- The nasal cannula is easy to apply and does not interfere with the clients ability to eat or talk.

- It also is relatively comfortable, permits some freedom of movement and is well tolerated by the client.
- It delivers a relatively low concentration of oxygen (24% to 45%) at flow rates of 2-6 L per minute
- Limitations of the cannula include inability to deliver higher concentration of oxygen and that it can be drying and irritating to mucous membranes.

2. Face mask: Face masks that cover the client's nose and mouth may be used for oxygen inhalation. Exhalation ports on the sides of the mask allow exhaled carbon dioxide to escape. A variety of oxygen masks are marked.

- The simple face mask delivers oxygen concentrations from 40% to 60% at litre flows of 5-8 L per minute, respectively.
- The partial rebreather mask delivers oxygen concentrations of 60% to 90% at litre flows of 6-10 L per minute, respectively. The oxygen reservoir bag that is attached allows the client to rebreath about the first third of the exhaled air in conjunction with oxygen. Thus it increases the FiO_2 by recycling expired oxygen. The partial rebreather bag must not totally deflate during inspiration to avoid carbon dioxide build up. If the problem occurs the nurse increases the litre flow of oxygen.
- The non rebreather mask delivers the highest oxygen concentration possible 95% to 100% by means other than intubation or mechanical ventilation at litre flows of 10 to 15 L per minute. One way valves between the reservoir bag and the mask prevent the room air and the client's exhaled air from entering the bag so only the oxygen in the bag is inspired.

3.Face tent: Face tents can replace oxygen masks when masks are poorly tolerated by clients. Face tents provide varying concentrations of oxygen for example 30% to 50% concentration of oxygen at 4 to 8 litre per minute. Frequently inspect the client's facial skin for dampness or chafing and dryness and treat as needed.

As with face masks the client's facial skin must be kept dry

4. Oxygen hood: An oxygen hood is used for babies who can breathe on their own but still need extra oxygen. A hood is a plastic dome or box with warm, moist oxygen inside. The hood is placed over the baby's head.

5. Oxygen tent: Consists of a canopy over the patient's bed that may cover the patient fully or partially and is connected to supply of oxygen.

Q 17. Steam inhalation .

- **DEFINITION:** Deep breathing of warm and moist air (vapour) into the lungs for local effect on the air passages or for a systemic effect.
- **PURPOSES:**
- To relieve the inflammation and congestion of the mucous membranes of the respiratory tract and Para nasal sinuses thus to produce symptomatic relief in acute and chronic sinusitis
- To soften thick tenacious mucus which helps in its expulsion from the respiratory tract
- To provide moisture and heat and to prevent dryness of the mucous membranes of the lungs and upper respiratory passages following operation such as tracheostomy
- To aid in absorption of oxygen
- To relieve spastic conditions of the larynx and bronchi
- To provide antiseptic action on the respiratory tract e.g. by using menthol, eucalyptus and tincture benzoin
- **ARTICLES:** Tray containing:
- Towel
- Nelson's inhaler
- Sputum cup with antiseptic solution
- Inhaler mouthpiece
- Gauze piece
- Cotton balls
- Ounce glass
- Face towel

- Kidney tray
- Cardiac table
- Pillows
- Medication like tincture benzoin if ordered
- Boiling water (160 degree F)

Q 18. Nebulization

= **DEFINITION:** Process of dispersing liquid medication into microscopic particles (aerosol) and delivering into lungs as patient inhales.

- **PURPOSES:**
- To administer medications directly into respiratory tract for sputum expectoration
- To reduce difficulty in bringing out thick tenacious respiratory secretions
- To increase vital capacity (he greatest volume of air that can be expelled from the lungs after taking the deepest possible breath.)
- To relieve dyspnoea
- **ARTICLES:**
- Nebulizer
- Medication and saline solution
- Sterile water
- Cotton balls
- Face mask (Nebulizer mask)
- Sputum cup with disinfectant
- Disposable tissues
- Kidney tray

Q 19 . Discuss the nurse's responsibility in oxygen administration

= Check the name, bed number and other identification of the patient

- Check the diagnosis and the need for oxygen therapy
- Check the doctors order for the initiation of the therapy, the dosage etc
- Check the doctors order for the specific precautions regarding the movement & positioning of the patient
- Assess the patient for any sign of clinical analysis e.g. cyanosis
- Check the patients vital signs
- Check the results of arterial blood gas analysis
- Check the patients mental status and the ability to follow instructions
- Check the articles available in the unit. Check O_2 cylinder for its accessories and their working condition.

Q 19. CPR

= Cardiopulmonary resuscitation (CPR) is a combination of techniques, including chest compressions, designed to pump the heart to get blood circulating and deliver oxygen to the brain until definitive treatment can stimulate the heart to start working again.

- CPR is a combination of rescue breathing & chest compressions delivered to victims thought to be in cardiac arrest.(Cardiac arrest is a sudden stop in effective blood flow due to the failure of the heart to contract effectively. Symptoms include loss of consciousness and abnormal or absent breathing. Some people may have chest pain, shortness of breath, or nausea before this occurs. If not treated within minutes, death usually occurs)
- CPR can support small amount of blood flow to heart & brain to 'take time' until normal heart function is restored.
- Permanent brain damage occurs if oxygen supply is stopped for more than 6 min.
- CPR alone is unlikely to restart the heart. Its main purpose is to restore partial flow of oxygenated blood to the brain and heart. The objective is to delay tissue death and to extend the brief window of opportunity for a successful resuscitation without permanent brain damage

CPR: Procedure:

- Before starting CPR, check
- Consciousness of person
- If no response, shake shoulder or give painful stimuli

CPR Table
Ratio
Rate (Beats/min)
Depth

Adult
1 breaths / 15 compressions
100 beats/min
1.5-2 inches
Child (1-8 Year)
1 breath / 5 compressions
100 beats/min
1-1.5 inches
Infant
1 breath / 5 compressions
100 + beats/min
1.5 inches

Spell C-A-B (In 2010 AHA changed its acronym of ABC to CAB i.e. Circulation, Airway, Breathing to perform CPR.)

- Remove person from any immediate danger.
- Check for spinal injury.
- Position person supine on firm surface.
- Kneel next to the person's neck or shoulders.
- Place heal of one hand over center of person's chest, between nipples, place other hand on the top of first hand.
- Keep elbow straight & position shoulders directly above hands.
- Compression consists of thrust which compresses heart & release which allows heart to refill with blood.
- These compressions are delivered at the rate of approx 100/min.

- Push hard & fast to make sure adequate depth & rate of compressions are maintained.
- When performing compressions, elbow should be locked & push straight down.
- Use enough force to push casualty's sternum down 1.5 – 2 inches (4-5cms).
- Release pressure completely so that sternum resumes its normal position, but do not remove heel of hand from compression site.

Q 20 .Methods Collection of urine specimen for culture

= Elimination may be defined as the removal of waste material from the body like urine, faeces, sweat, discharge etc through the intestine, kidneys, lungs skin.

- **Method of collecting single urine specimen or random specimens:**
- It means the amount of urine voided at a time.
- Usually morning specimens are collected.
- 100-200ml of urine will be sufficient for usual tests.
- After cleaning the genital area, the patient passes urine into a clean urinal or a clean kidney tray or directly into specimen bottle, taking care not to spill the urine on the outside of the container.
- **Method of collecting midstream specimen:**
- Ask the patient to clean the genital area with soap and water, and then rinse with water alone.
- In female patients the labia are separated for cleaning and kept apart until the urine has been collected.
- In male patients the foreskin should be retracted and the glans penis is cleaned before the collection of the urine.
- The patient begins to void into the toilet, commode or bed pan. Then the patient stops the stream of urine, sterile container is positioned and continues to void into the container. When enough urine has been voided for the specimen the patient stops the stream again, the container is removed and then finishes

voiding in the original receptacle. By this method the first stream of urine flushes out the organism and mucus usually present at the meatus, so that accurate result can be obtained.

- **Method of collecting catheter specimen:**
- As far as possible the catheterization is avoided as it may cause urinary infection due to the introduction of microorganism along with the catheter into the urinary tract or it may cause tissue trauma.
- Straight catheter of small size is inserted into bladder under aseptic conditions, allowing urine flowing directly into the sterile specimen container.
- Specimen may also be collected from the catheter or drainage tubing of indwelling catheter. Most urinary drainage system has a specimen collection port built into the top of the drainage tubing. This self sealing rubber covered area is cleansed and the urine is aspirated with sterile needle and syringe. If there is no collection port and the catheter is not elastic, use a small gauge (25) needle and syringe to aspirate urine from the catheter itself.
- **Method of collecting 24 hours urine specimen:**
- The collection of urine begins at 6AM.
- Ask the patient to void at 6AM and discard the whole urine.
- All the subsequent voiding should be measured and collected in the bottle which is labelled.
- Continue till 6AM of next morning.
- It is necessary to add preservatives to the urine to prevent decomposition and multiplication of bacteria. A variety of preservatives are available such as boric acid, formalin, chloroform etc.

Q 21. SCIENTIFIC PRINCIPLES IN URINE TESTING
= ANATOMY AND PHYSIOLOGY:

- The urinary system consists of two kidneys, two ureters, the urinary bladder and the urethra

- The kidneys are the glandular organs that secrete urine from the blood
- The kidneys help to maintain the proper fluid and electrolyte balance in the body
- Ureters convey the urine from the kidneys to the bladder
- The bladder is a hollow muscular organ and serves as a reservoir for urine. It expels urine by contraction from the body through urethra
- The urethra is a small tube about one forth inch in diameter and about one and one half inches long in female and eight or nine inches long in male
- The bladder is lined with mucous membrane which continues to the urethra, the ureters and the pelvis of the kidney
- When about 300 ml of urine is accumulated in the bladder, there is a urge to void it
- The usual daily amount of urine secreted by a normal adult is 1200 to 1500ml
- The urine is retained in the bladder by an internal sphincter which is located at the opening of the bladder into the urethra
- In the female it is located between the clitoris and the vaginal opening.

2. **MICROBIOLOGY** ; If an infection is present in the one part of urinary tract, it may travel to another part because the mucous membrane is continuous from the urethra up to the pelvis of the kidney

The urinary tract gives favourable condition to multiply the micro organisms because the tract is dark moist and warm

Cystitis may occur due to highly concentrated urine or by irritating drugs used in the irrigation and instillation by bacteria, by injury, or by obstruction of the flow of urine

Colon bacillus commonly causes the urinary infection

The staphylococci, the streptococci, the gonococci, the typhoid bacilli and the tuberclebacilli are responsible for bladder infection

3) physical and chemical

- If a large quantity of urine collects in the bladder , pressure on adjacent organs may cause pain
- Heat is carried to organs and tissues adjacent to the bladder by conduction through tissues
- The hot water bag may be applied over the lower abdomen or a warm solution poured over vulva to give warmth
- Cold contracts tissue, so cool water should be used over the vulva or putting the hands in the cold water will help in contracting the bladder muscle to produce urination
- Urine contains about 95% of water and 3.7% organic and 1.3% inorganic wastes
- The odour of fresh urine is faintly aromatic
- The specific gravity of urine is slightly acidic pH below 7
- Creatinine is found in the normal urine of adult
- Some drugs may be excreted by the kidneys and found in the urine
- Hot water and some chemicals coagulate protein so urine is heated for albumin test or nitric acid is used to test the urine for albumin
- Phosphates dilute in the acetic acid
- Benedict solution is used to test the urine for sugar.

4) pharmacology :

- Drugs which increase the flow of urine are called diuretics
- Drugs which decrease the flow of urine are called anti diuretics

5 . Physiology :

- Certain psychic states greatly increase the tonicity of the muscles of the bladder so that internal pressure and the desire to urination is increased
- Explain the purpose to the patient to get the co-operation

Q 22. Enlist the different types of enema

= An enema is a solution introduced into the rectum and large intestine. The action of an enema is to distend the intestine and sometimes to irritate the intestinal mucosa, thereby increasing peristalsis and the excretion of feces and flatus

- **Cleansing enema:**
- Cleansing enemas are intended to remove feces. They are given chiefly to:

- Prevent the escape of faces during surgery
- Prepare the intestine for certain diagnostic tests such as X ray or visualization tests (e.g. colonoscopy)
- Remove feces in instances of constipation or impaction

- There are three types of cleansing enemas: the large volume enema, the small volume enema and the packaged disposable enema
- **Carminative enema:**
- It is also called antispasmodic enema.
- It is given to relieve gaseous distention of abdomen by increasing peristalsis and expulsion of flatus
- The solution used is 8 to16 ml of turpentine mixed thoroughly with 600 to 1200 ml of soap solution
- For an adult 60-80 ml of fluid is instilled.
- **Retention enema:** A retention enema introduces oil or medication into the rectum and sigmoid colon.
- The liquid is retained for a relatively long period (e.g. 1 to 3 hours).
- An oil retention enema acts to soften the feces and to lubricate the rectum and anal canal, thus facilitating passage of the feces. This enema is usually followed by a cleansing enema.
- Antibiotic enemas are used to treat infections locally, antihelmentic enemas to kill helminths such as worms and intestinal parasites and nutritive enemas to administer fluids and

nutrients to the rectum.

- **OIL ENEMA:**
- It is given to soften fecal matter in cases of severe constipation. The enema must be retained ½ or 1 hour to soften the feces
- The solutions used are olive oil, castor oil
- The amount of solution used is 115 to 175 ml
- The temperature of the solution is 100 degree F
- **Antihelmentic enema:**
- It is given to destroy and expel worms from the intestines
- Cleansing enema must be given prior to antihelmentic enema so that the drug comes in direct contact with worms and lining of intestine
- The solution used is hypertonic saline solution sodium chloride 60ml with 600ml of water
- The amount of solution give is 250ml
- **Cold enema:**
- Cold enema or ice water enema is given to reduce body temperature in hyper pyrexia and heat stroke.
- It is given in the form of colonic irrigations
- The temperature of the solution is 80-90degree F
- **Astringent enema:**
- Astringent enema contracts the tissues and blood vessels , checks bleeding and inflammation , lessens the amount of mucus discharge and gives a temporary relief in the inflamed area
- It is usually given in colitis and dysentery
- The solution used are tannic acid 25gm to 600 ml water, alum 30gm to 600ml of water and silver nitrate 2% (silver nitrate is dissolved in the distilled water)
- **Sedative enema:**
- Sedative enema contains an anesthetic drug to produce anesthesia in the patient. The commonly used drug is paraldehyde
- Dose is given as per doctors order
- **Emollient enema:**

- Emollient enema or starch enema is given in case of diarrhea to relieve irritation in an inflamed mucus membrane
- The solution used is starch and opium- Tr. Opium 1-2ml added to 120 to 180 ml of starch mucilage or rice water
- The temperature of the solution is 100 to 105 F
- **Nutrient enema:**
- It is given to supply food and fluids to the body
- Selection of the fluids depends upon the ability of the colon to absorb it
- Nutrient enema is particularly useful in conditions like hemophilia
- The solution used are normal saline, glucose saline
- The amount of solution used is 110-1700ml in 24 hours or 180 to 270 ml at 4 hourly interval
- The temperature of solution is 100 degree F

Q 23 . Explain composition and characteristics of urine

= ABNORMAL CONSTITUENT OF URINEüCHEMICAL COMPOSITION OF URINE MAIN TERMS ASSOSIATED WITH URINE COMPOSITION PHYSICAL CHARACTERISTIC OF URINE COLOUR ODOUR TURBIDITY PH VOLUME DENSITY (Specific Gravity) ü

URINE•Urine is a liquid product of the body secreted by kidney Through the process is called urination (micturition) Excreted through urethra •Cellular metabolism generates numerous by product , (rich in nitrogen) that require clearence from the blood stream as urination •Urination is the primary method for excreting water soluble chemicals from the body •Human urine with human faecus are collectively called human waste

COMPOSITION OF URINE● 95% of volume of normal urine is due to water Organic components: ● urea ● urobilinogen ● uric acid ● creatinine ● amino acids ● metabolites of hormones Inorganic components: ● cations: $Na+$, $K+$, $Ca2+$, $NH4$ + ● anions: $Cl-$, $SO4$ 2-, $HCO3$ -, $HPO4$ -

Turbidity or cloudiness may be caused by excessive cellular material or protein in the urineüIf the sample contained many red blood cells, it would be cloudy as well as red. üA red or red-brown (abnormal) color could be from a food dye, eating fresh beets, a drug, or the presence of either hemoglobin or myoglobin. üConcentrated urine has a deeper yellow/amber color üClear, pale to deep yellow (due to urochrome) üColor and transparency

Pinkish urine can result from the consumption of beetü brown urine can be a symptoms of jaundice,rhabdomylosis or gilberts syndrome ü Orange urine is also form at certain medication such as rifamine ü Yellow ,orange colour is due to the removal of b vitamin ü Dark yellow urine is often indicative of hydration ü

Consumption of alchohol,saffron cofee,tunafis and onion can result in teltate scents...§Elevated ketones smells fruity or acetone-like §Some drugs and vegetables (asparagus) alter the usual odor § Standing urine develops an ammonia odor §Fresh urine is slightly aromatic §Odor

PH -5.5 – 6.8 Acidic – meat food, diabetes mellitus, starvation, fever Alkaline – plant food, cystitis, pyelitis

•Acidic urine contribute to the formation of stones of uric acid (kidneys,ureter,bladders) •Diet with citrus ,vegetables and dairy product increase urine ph(more basic) •Diet with meat,cranberries,druds, will decrease urine ph(more acidic)

Volume •Average urine production in humanis about 1-2 L per day •Volume is depending on the state of hydration,activity level,environmental factor,and health of the individual Density • Density of the urine ranges between 1.003-1.035 g cm^-3

ANURIA : COMPLETE STOPPAGE OF URINE OLIGURIA :REDUCED AMOUNT OF URINE POLYURIA :INCREASED AMOUNT OF URINE NOCTURIA :INCREASED AMOUNT OF URINE @ NIGHT

• Urine is 95% water and 5% solutes • Nitrogenous wastes include urea, uric acid, and creatinine • Other normal solutes include: • Sodium, potassium, phosphate, and sulfate ions • Calcium, magnesium, and bicarbonate ions • Abnormally high concentrations of any urinary constituents may indicate pathology

Q 24 List the physiological effect of hot and cold applications and purposes

= physiological Effects of Hot Applications

1. Peripheral vasodilatations.
2. Increased capillary permeability.
3. Increased local metabolism.
4. Increased oxygen consumption.
5. Blood-flow is increased.
6. Motility of leukocytes increase.
7. Muscle tone increased.

Purposes :

- Heat decreases pain.
- To provide comfort.
- To promote circulation.
- To relax the muscles.
- To promote healing.
- To relieve deep congestion.
- To soften the exudates.
- To counteract sudden drop in temperature.
- To decrease joint stiffness.
- To relieve bladder distention.

Physiological effect of cold applications

1.peripheral vasoconstriction

2.decrease capillary permeability

3.decrease cellular metabolism

4. decrease oxygen consumption

5.decrease muscle tone

6. anesthesia and slowed conduction

Purposes :

- cold relieves pain
- It prevent from gangrene

- to prevent inflammation
- to prevent edema
- to arrest bleeding
- to decrease the elevated body temperature to anesthetize an area
- to provide comfort

Q 25. Write principles of body mechanics

= Body mechanics are the coordinated efforts of the musculoskeletal and nervous systems to maintain balance, posture and body alignment during lifting, bending, moving and performing ADLs.

- Body mechanics is the efficient use of the body as a machine and as a means of locomotion.

PRINCIPLES OF BODY MECHANICS

- When planning a transfer or move, free the surrounding area of obstacles
- The wider the base of support and lower the centre of gravity, greater is the stability of the nurse
- The lower the centre of gravity the greater the stability of the nurse
- The equilibrium of an object is maintained as long as the line of gravity passes through its base of support
- Facing the direction of movement prevents abnormal twisting of the spine.
- Dividing balanced activity between arms and legs reduces the risk of back injury
- Rolling, turning or pivoting requires less work than lifting
- When friction is reduced between the object to be moved and the surface on which it is moved, less force is required to move it.
- Reducing the force of work reduces the risk of injury

- The greater the preparatory contraction of the muscles before moving an object the lesser will be the energy required to move it and lesser the likelihood of strain and injury.
- Maintaining good body mechanics reduces fatigue of the muscle groups
- Alternating periods of rest and activity helps to reduce fatigue
- Continuous muscle exertion can result in muscle strain, injury and fatigue.

Q 26 . Discuss importance of body mechanics for nurses while caring for clients

= **IMPORTANCE OF BODY MECHANICS**

- Proper body alignment and posture prevent fatigue and deformities
- It promotes physiological function of the body
- It aids in circulation and digestion
- It minimizes the expenditure of energy
- It helps in maintaining balance of body without any strain and spasm resulting in backache
- It helps in maintaining size and shape of thoracic, abdominal and pelvic cavities and thus prevents kyphosis, lordosis, scoliosis etc.
- It contributes to one's beauty

Q 27. Care of pressure points.

= 1. Identification of clients who are particularly prone to the development of decubitus ulcer.

2. Confirm the high risk patients and daily examination for the signs and symptoms.

3. Relieve pressure by using special mattress, beds and comfort devices.

4. Change position of the client every 2 hourly and give back care all bedridden patients.

5. Loosening tight bandages and restraints.

6. Avoid friction by providing smooth, firm and wrinkle free bed, keep the bottom clothes

free from crumbs and foreign bodies.

7. Keep the patient clean and dry. Prevent moisture by changing linen when, it is wet or

soiled.

8. Giving back care to patients immediately following micturition and defecation.

9. Avoid physical or mechanical injury to the skin from improper fitting of prosthesis or

from burns caused by excessively hot or cold applications.

10. Use a bed cradle to lift the weight of bed linen off the patient to enable him or her to

move in bed freely.

11. Supply well balanced diet and adequate fluids to maintain general health of the patient

Q 28. Chest physiotherapy

= Definition • Chest physiotherapy (CPT) is a group of therapies for mobilizing pulmonary secretions. These therapies include chest percussion, vibration and postural drainage. • CPT is followed by productive coughing or suctioning of a patient who has a decreased ability to cough. • This is especially helpful for patients with large amount of secretions or ineffective cough.

1. Indications: • It is indicated for patients in whom cough is insufficient to clear thick, tenacious, or localized secretions. • Examples: • Cystic fibrosis • Bronchiectasis • Atelctasis • Lung abscess • Pneumonia
2. Contraindications • Increased ICP • Unstable head or neck injury • Active hemorrhage or hemoptysis • Recent spinal injury • Rib fracture • Flail chest • Uncontrolled hypertension • Anticoagulation • Thoracic surgeries
3. Assessment for Chest Physiotherapy • Assess the vital signs • Know the patient's medications. Certain medications, particularly diuretics antihypertensive cause fluid and

haemodynamic changes. These decrease patient's tolerance to positional changes and postural drainage • Assess for any contra indications

4. Assessment for Chest Physiotherapy • Perform detailed physical examination of the chest • Review the patients X-ray and other blood investigations.
5. Techniques in Chest Physiotherapy • Chest physiotherapy consists of three techniques: 1. Percussion / Clapping/ Cupping 2. Vibration 3. Postural Drainage
6. Percussion / Clapping • Chest percussion involves rhythmically clapping on the chest wall over the area being drained to force secretions into larger airways for expectoration. • Position the hand so the fingers and thumb touch and the hands are cupped.
7. Percussion
8. Percussion • Perform chest percussion by vigorously striking the chest wall alternately with cupped hands. • The procedure should produce a hollow sound and should not be painful. • Perform percussion over a single layer of clothing, not over butt
9. Percussion • Percussion is contraindicated in patients with bleeding disorders, osteoporosis, fractured ribs and open wounds and surgeries. • Don't percuss over the spine, sternum, stomach or lower back as trauma can occur to the spleen, liver, or kidneys. • Typically, each area is percussed for 30 to 6o seconds several times a day. • If the patient has tenacious secretions, the area must be percussed for 3-5 minutes several times per day.
10. Vibration • Vibration is a gentle, shaking pressure applied to the chest wall to move secretions into larger airways. • The nurse uses rhythmic contractions and relaxations of arm and shoulder muscles over the patient's chest. • During vibration, place your flat hand firmly against the chest wall, on the appropriate lung segment to be drained.

CHAPTER ELEVEN

UNIT 11: INFECTION CONTROL IN CLINICAL SETTING

SHORT ANSWER QUESTION

Q 1. Barrier nursing

= **Barrier nursing** is a largely archaic term for a set of stringent infection control techniques used in **nursing**. The aim of **barrier nursing** is to protect medical staff against infection by patients and also protect patients with highly infectious diseases from spreading their pathogens to other non-infected people.

isolation technique

- Isolation technique is intended to confine the microorganisms within a given and recognized area.
- There are number of isolation techniques and precautions used to prevent the spread of infection.
- These are-

1. Respiratory isolation
2. Enteric isolation
3. Wound and skin isolation
4. Blood isolation

respiratory isolation

- Respiratory isolation is indicated in situations where the pathogens are spread on droplet from respiratory tract. In this type of isolation mask are generally worn by nurses.
- Gowns are also one when carrying for the small infants and because of the possibilities of drooling by the infants.
- Clients are taught to cover their noses and mouths with several layers of tissue paper or handkerchief.
- Restrict the numbers of visitors.
- Precautions must be taken while collecting sputum specimen from the clients when attending to client with respiratory infection.
- The nurse should keep a reasonable distance to prevent the droplet infection and to prevent breathing contaminated air.
- The nurse suffering from respiratory disease should not attend to the client

enteric isolation

- Enteric isolation is indicated when the pathogens are transmitted in faces.
- For this type of isolation gloves and gown be worn while handling soiled articles.
- Thorough hand washing should be emphasized by both clients and nurses.
- excreta maybe disinfectant by adding line before disposal

Wound and skin isolation

- In this type of isolation is for pathogens which are found in wound and can be transmitted by the contact within wound or by contact with the article contaminated with the wonder discharge.
- Usually gowns and gloves are worn in this type of infection.
- Important points to remember is the safeguard disposal of dressing and discharge from the wound.

- Disinfection of article
- Strict isolation technique should be followed while caring for client with abscess was infected burn, scabies etc.
- All the article used for this client should be kept separate.

blood isolation

- This type of isolation is intended to prevent transmission of pathogens that are found in the blood.
- Therefore any equipment that comes in contact with the clients blood should be carefully disinfectant before touching another object or person.
- Use of gloves are also emphasize to prevent this type of infection

General precaution

- maintain high degree of cleanliness
- health teaching: the client and his relative are to be taught about the spread of infection and its prevention
- Minimize the numbers of visitors: children under 10 years should not allowed to enter into the hospital wards.
- Emphasize on hand washing: washing hand after elimination, before eating and after handling the client or his article
- Toilet article separate for each person
- all personal caring for the sick and also that public should have the immunization against communicable diseases
- Person with lower resistance (example client with anemia) should be protected
- as far as possible the client should be nursed in the separate room.
- if separate rooms are not available there should be at least a sufficient space in between the beds.

Q 2. Standard safety precautions/ Universal precautions

= Previously called standard Precautions.

- Universal precaution are control guidelines designed to protect workers from exposure to Diseases spread by Blood and other Body fluids.
    - Standard precautions are designed to reduce the **risk of transmission** of blood borne and other pathogens from both recognized and unrecognized sources to a susceptible host.
    - They are the basic level of **infection control** precaution.
- Applied universally in caring for all patients.
    - Hand washing
    - Wearing protective items
    - Decontamination of equipment and devices
    - Use and disposal of needles and sharps safely (no recapping)
    - Prompt cleaning up of blood and body fluid spills
    - Systems for safe collection of waste and disposal

1. Hand washing

- Hand washing is the most important method of disease prevention.
- Bacteria and bacteria can be spread via dirty hands and the are too small to see with the human eye.

wash hands properly in order to remove them.

2. Use of Personal Protective Equipment

- Gloves
- Aprons
- Gowns
- Protective eyewear
- Face shields
- Masks

Use of Mask, Cap, Eye Wear

- Will certainly protect us from splashes of Blood or Body fluids.
- Don't underestimate the importance of Use of Cap and Mask.
- It equally protects our patients.

Use of Gloves

Use of a pair of disposable plastic gloves can protect if chances of contact with Blood or Body fluid is anticipated/inevitable.

Use of Foot wear

- Wearing foot wear covering entire sole protects the entry of Microbes from the contaminated floors with Blood and Body fluids.
- Remember many of us have cracks on our feet.

4. Decontamination of equipment and devices

- All equipment will require cleaning. Some equipment will also require disinfecting or sterilizing.
- The choice of method also depends on the purpose of the equipment and other risk factors.
- Cleaning and/or disinfection of medical equipment must:

1. Take place after and between uses on individual service users.
2. Once cleaned/disinfected, pieces of equipment should be labeled with an appropriate tag to identify that it has been cleaned.
3. Audits should be carried out regularly on cleanliness of equipment in each area.
4. Equipment requiring service or repair must be thoroughly cleaned and decontaminated prior to inspection and a label attached identifying method of decontamination.

4.Use and disposal of needles and sharps safely (no recapping)

- Proper handling and disposal of needles.
- Taking precautions to prevent injury from scalpels, needles, and other sharp instruments.

5 . Dealing with Needle stick Injuries

Consider all Needle stick injuries as a serious health hazard in the era of AIDS

All events of Needle stick injuries to be reported to the supervisory staff.

Wash the injured areas with soap and water.

Encourage bleeding if any.

Prophylaxis for prevention of HIV/HBV is top priority.

Anti retroviral prophylaxis, if necessary should started within 2 hours, (if injury is from HIV positive or high risk group).

6 Spillage of Blood/Body fluids

- A common health hazard in the working environment.
- Never wipe the spillage with working wet mop.

Always cover the spills with paper and pour 1 % Hypochlorite or Bleaching

powder to decontaminate the spills with HIV/HBV virus.

Q 3. Medical asepsis and surgical asepsis

= The term asepsis means the absence of disease-producing microorganisms.

Sum total of the effort to keep the patient's environment free from contamination and the patient free from colonizationn .Reducing the number of microbes to an irreducible number.

Sl. No.	FEATURE	MEDICAL ASEPSIS	SURGICAL ASEPSIS
1	**Goal**	Medical asepsis refers to all practical used in prevention of cross infection	Surgical asepsis refers to all practices used to keep objects completely sterile.
2	**Technique**	In medical asepsis a clean technique is used	In surgical asepsis a sterile technique is used.
3	**Hand Washing**	Hands are washed for at least 30 seconds	Hands should be cleaned thoroughly for at least 3 to 5 minutes (In operating room hands are scrubbed up to 10 minutes).
4	**Contaminated Area**	Hands are considered to be more contaminated than elbows.	Elbows are considered to be more contaminated than hands.
5	**Water Flow**	Water should flow from the area of least contamination (elbow) to the area more contaminated (hands).	Water should flow from hands to elbow.
6	**Growing Technique**	• Isolation gowns are used when caring for a infectious patient. • Isolation gowns are disposable	• Sterile gowns are used in the operating room, delivery room and when ever open wounds are present which needs a sterile technique. • Sterile gowns are reusable after sterilization of contaminated gown.
7	**Sterilization Technique**	Sterilization techniques not used	Surgical asepsis= Medical asepsis + Sterilization technique.
8	**Care of Articles**	Disinfection technique is used. • Cleaning of isolation units daily. • Disinfection of all the articles using disinfectant • Safe disposal of excreta.	Sterilization technique is used. • Boiling • Cold sterilization • Fumigation • UV light sterilization • Steam under pressure or autoclaving.

Medical asepsis and surgical asepsis

Q 4. Nosocomial infection

= Defination : **Hospital-acquired infection** (HAI)/nosocomial infection — is an infection that is contracted from the environment or staff of a healthcare facility.

Sources of Infection

- **Endogenous:**

§ Patients own flora may invade patient's tissue during some surgical

operations or instrumental manipulations

§ Normal commensals of the skin, respiratory, GI, UG tract

- **Exogenous:**

§ From another patient / staff member / environment in the hospital

§ Environmental sources: Inanimate objects, air, water, food

§ Cross infection from: other patients, hospital staff (suffering from
infections or asymptomatic carriers)

Modes of Transmission

- **1. Contact:**

Most common route of transmission

— **Hands or Clothing:**

- Hands of staff: important vehicle of spread
- Contact of hands & clothing of attendants

Eg: *Staphylococcus aureus, Streptococcus pyrogenes*

— **Inanimate objects:**

- Improper disinfection of Instruments: endoscope, bronchoscope,
cystoscope

Eg: *Pseudomonas aeruginosa*

- **2. Airborne:**

— **Droplets:**

- Droplets of Respiratory infections: transmitted by inhalation

— **Dust:**

- Dust from bedding, floors, wound exudates & skin

Eg: *Pseudomonas aeruginosa, Staphylococcus aureus*

— Aerosols:

- Aerosols from nebulizers, humidifiers & AC

Eg: *Legionella pneumophila*

- **3.Oral Route:**

- Hospital food may contain Antibiotic-resistant bacteria → may colonize intestine → can cause infections

- **4. Parenteral route:**

- Disposable syringes & needles

- Certain infections may be transmitted by blood transfusion, tissue donation, contaminated blood products

Eg: Hepatitis B, HIV

Types of hospital acquired infection

- **bloodstream infection** -this include bacteria and septicemia they are generally caused by introduction of intravascular catheter cannulas.
- **Pneumonia** -ventilator associated pneumonia(VAP) in ICU patient patients with prior respiratory tract pathology smokers patient who have undergone abdominal of thoracic surgery are usually affected.
- **Urinary tract infection** it is usually caused by introduction of eggs in organisms urinary tract catheter for urinary tract instrumentation.
- **Gastrointestinal infection** it can occur by consumption of contaminated food and cause food poisoning manifested by vomiting diarrhea or dysentery.
- **Skin and soft tissue infection** it can occurred by surgical procedure and contamination of wound and secondary infection of traumatic wound example of positive microorganisms

Q 5. Biomedical waste management

= Any **waste** which is generated during the diagnosis , treatment and immunization of human beings or animals or in research activities pertaining thereto or in the production or testing of biological.

Classification of biomedical waste :

1 . **Infectious waste :** Infectious waste is suspected to contain pathogens (bacteria , viruses, parasites, or fungi.) In sufficient quantity to cause diseases in a susceptible host .

2 . **Pathological waste :** it contains tissue, organs , body parts , and animal blood, human foetuses, body fluids.

3 . **3. SHARPS:**

These are the items that could cause cuts or puncture wounds, including;

- Needles,
- Scalpel and other blades,
- Knives,
- Infusion sets,
- Saws,
- Broken glass, and nails.

4.PHARMACEUTICAL WASTE:

It includes expired, unused, spilt, and contaminated

- Pharmaceutical products,
- Drugs,
- Vaccines, and sera
- **5. GENOTOXIC WASTE:**

- Genotoxic waste is hazardous and may have;

- Mutagenic,
- Teratogenic, or
- Carcinogenic properties.

6. CHEMICAL WASTE:

It consists of discarded

- Solid,
- Liquid, and

- Gaseous chemicals

Chemical waste may be hazardous or nonhazardous.

It is considered to be hazardous if it has at least one of the following properties:

- Toxic,
- Corrosive (acids of pH < 2 and bases of pH> 12)
- Flammable,
- Reactive

7. WASTES WITH HIGH CONTENT OF HEAVY METALS:

It represents a subcategory of hazardous chemical waste, and is usually highly toxic.

It includes

- Batteries,
- Broken thermometer,
- Blood-pressure gauges.

8. PRESSURIZED CONTAINERS:

Many types of gas are used in health care, and are often stored in pressurized cylinders, cartridges, and aerosol cans.

Most common gases used in health care includes:

- **Anesthetic gases**
- **Oxygen**
- **Compressed air**
- **9. RADIOACTIVE WASTE:**
- It includes the X- rays, α- and β- particles, and γ- rays emitted by radioactive substances.

Q 6 . Explain in detail about the methods of sterilization. (15 marks)

= Sterilization: Sterilization is a process by which an article, surface or medium is freed of all living microorganisms including viruses, bacteria ,their spores & fungi.

Sterile: Material is heated in such a way that it contains no living organisms is said to be sterile.

METHODS OF STERILISATION

THE VARIOUS METHODS USED IN STERILISATION CAN BE CLASSIFIED AS BELOW:

1. PHYSICAL METHODS :

a) Sunlight

b) Drying

c) Heat : Dry heat , Moist heat .

- **Temperature below 100 c**
- **Temperature at 100 c**
- **Temperature above 100 c**

d) filteration

e) Radiation

f) Sonic and ultra sonic vibrations

2. Chemical Methods:

a. Alcohols
b. Aldehydes
c. Dyes
d. Halogens
e. Phenols
f. Surface active agents
g. Metallic salts
h. Gases

<u>I. Physical methods</u>

<u>1.SUNLIGHT:</u>

- Direct sunlight has sterilizing effect due to combined effect of UV rays & heat rays.
- It has bactericidal effect & is one of the natural methods of sterilization of water in rivers , lakes & tanks.
- It is used to sterilize blankets, beddings, clothes, utensils, bedpans, etc.
- It is experimentally proved that typhoid bacilli when exposed to the sun on piece of white drill cloth were killed in two hours, whereas bacteria remain alive in dark even after six days.
- **2.DRYING OR DESICCATION:**
- Moisture is essential for the growth of bacteria, so drying in air has deleterious effect on many bacteria.
- However spores are unaffected & can remain alive for several months or even years.
- Therefore, it **is not an ideal method** of sterilization
- **3.HEAT**
- Most common and one of the most effective methods of sterilization. Factors influencing sterilization by heat are : -
- i. Nature of heat
- a. Dry
- b. Moist
- ii. Temperature & time
- iii. No. of organism present
- iv. Characteristics of organism such as species& sporing capacity.
- v. Type of material from which organism is to be eradicated

6.IRRADIATION

Radiation used for sterilization is of two types

1. Ionizing radiation, e.g., X-rays, gamma rays, and high speed electrons .
2. Non-ionizing radiation, e.g. ultraviolet light, and infrared light.

These forms of radiation can be used to kill or inactivate microorganisms.

1. **Ionizing Radiation**

- X-rays, gamma rays and cosmic rays are highly lethal to DNA and other vital constituents.
- They have high penetration power.
- There is no appreciable increase in temperature, thus referred to as **cold sterilization**.
- Commercial plants use gamma radiation for sterilizing plastics, syringes, swabs, catheters etc.

.

2. Non-ionizing radiation

Two types of non-ionizing radiations are used for sterilization:-

a. Ultraviolet -

Short range UV(UVC) is considered **"germicidal UV".**

At a wavelength of **2537 Angstroms** UV will destroy micro-organismal DNA.

Used mainly for air purification and water purification in hospitals.

b. Infrared –

It is most commonly used to purify air, such as in the operating room. Infrared is effective, however, it has no penetrating ability.

CHAPTER TWELVE

UNIT 12: ADMINISTRATION OF MEDICATION

SHORT ANSWER QUESTION

Q 1 . Nursing responsibility in medicine administration

= Nurses who administer medications are responsible for their own actions. Question any order that is illegible or that you consider incorrect. Call the person who prescribed the medication for clarification.

• Be knowledgeable about the medications you administer. You need to know why the client is receiving the medication. Look up the necessary information if you are not familiar with the medication.

• Federal laws govern the use of narcotics and barbiturates. Keep these medications in a locked place.

• Use only medications that are in a clearly labeled container.

• Do not use liquid medications that are cloudy or have changed color.

• Calculate drug doses accurately. If you are uncertain, ask another nurse to double-check your calculations.

• Administer only medications personally prepared.

• Before administering a medication, identify the client correctly using the appropriate means of identification, such as checking the identification bracelet.

- Do not leave medications at the bedside, with certain exceptions (e.g., nitroglycerin, cough syrup). Check agency policy.
- If a client vomits after taking an oral medication, report this to the nurse in charge, or the primary care provider, or both.
- Take special precautions when administering certain medications; for example, have another nurse check the dosages of anticoagulants, insulin, and certain IV preparations.
- Most hospital policies require new orders from the primary care provider for a client's postsurgery care.
- When a medication is omitted for any reason, record the fact together with the reason.
- When a medication error is made, report it immediately to the nurse in charge, the primary care provider, or both.
- Always check a medication's expiration date.

Q 2. Routes of drug administration

= ROUTES OF ADMINISTRATION

Pharmaceutical preparations are generally designed for one or two specific routes of administration (Table 35–5). The route of administration should be indicated when the drug is ordered. When administering a drug, the nurse should ensure that the pharmaceutical preparation is appropriate for the route specified.

Oral

Oral administration is the most common, least expensive, and most convenient route for most clients. In oral administration, the drug is swallowed. Because the skin is not broken as it is for an injection, oral administration is also a safe method.

The major disadvantages can include an unpleasant taste of the drugs, irritation of the gastric mucosa, irregular absorption from the

GI tract, slow absorption, and, in some cases, harm to the client's teeth. For example, the liquid preparation of ferrous sulfate (iron) can stain the teeth.

Sublingual

In sublingual administration a drug is placed under the tongue, where it dissolves (Figure 35–3 •). In a relatively short time, the drug is largely absorbed into the blood vessels on the underside of the tongue. The medication should not be swallowed. Nitroglycerin is one example of a drug commonly given in this manner

.

Buccal

Buccal means "pertaining to the cheek." In buccal administration, a medication (e.g., a tablet) is held in the mouth against the mucous membranes of the cheek until the drug dissolves (Figure 35–4 •). The drug may act locally on the mucous membranes of the mouth or systemically when it is swallowed in the saliva.

Parenteral

The parenteral route is defined as other than through the alimentary or respiratory tract; that is, by needle. The following are some of the more common routes for parenteral administration:

- Subcutaneous (hypodermic)—into the subcutaneous tissue, just below the skin
- Intramuscular (IM)—into a muscle
- Intradermal (ID)—under the epidermis (into the dermis)
- Intravenous (IV)—into a vein.

Some of the less commonly used routes for parenteral administration are intra-arterial (into an artery), intracardiac (into the heart

muscle), intraosseous (into a bone), intrathecal or intraspinal (into

the spinal canal), intrapleural (into the pleural space), epidural (into

the epidural space), and intra-articular (into a joint). Sterile equipment and sterile drug solution are essential for all parenteral therapy.

The main advantage is fast absorption.

Topical

Topical applications are those applied to a circumscribed surface

area of the body. They affect only the area to which they are applied.

Topical applications include the following:

- Dermatologic preparations—applied to the skin
- Instillations and irrigations—applied into body cavities or orifices,

such as the urinary bladder, eyes, ears, nose, rectum, or vagina

Inhalations—administered into the respiratory tract by a nebulizer or positive pressure breathing apparatus. Air, oxygen, and vapor are generally used to carry the drug into the lungs.

Q 3 . Rights of drug /principals of drug administration

= RIGHT MEDICATION

- The medication given was the medication ordered.

RIGHT DOSE

- The dose ordered is appropriate for the client.
- Give special attention if the calculation indicates multiple pills/ tablets or a large quantity of a liquid medication. This can be an indication that the math calculation may be incorrect.
- Double-check calculations that appear questionable.
- Know the usual dosage range of the medication.
- Question a dose outside of the usual dosage range.

RIGHT TIME

- Give the medication at the right frequency and at the time ordered according to agency policy.

• Medications should be given within the agency guidelines.

RIGHT ROUTE

• Give the medication by the ordered route.

• Make certain that the route is safe and appropriate for the client.

RIGHT CLIENT

• Medication is given to the intended client.

• Check the client's identification band with each administration of a medication.

• Know the agency's name alert procedure when clients with the same or similar last names are on the nursing unit.

RIGHT CLIENT EDUCATION

• Explain information about the medication to the client (e.g., why receiving, what to expect, any precautions).

RIGHT DOCUMENTATION

• Document medication administration after giving it, not before.

• If time of administration differs from prescribed time, note the time on the MAR and explain the reason and follow-through activities (e.g., pharmacy states medication will be available in 2 hours) in nursing notes.

• If a medication is not given, follow the agency's policy for documenting the reason why.

RIGHT TO REFUSE

• Adult clients have the right to refuse any medication.

• The nurse's role is to ensure that the client is fully informed of the potential consequences of refusal and to communicate the client's refusal to the health care provider.

RIGHT ASSESSMENT

• Some medications require specific assessments prior to administration (e.g., apical pulse, blood pressure, lab results).

• Medication orders may include specific parameters for administration (e.g., do not give if pulse less than 60 or systolic blood pressure less than 100).

RIGHT EVALUATION

• Conduct appropriate follow-up (e.g., was the desired effect achieved or not? Did the client experience any side effects or adverse reactions?).

Q 4. Purpose of medication Drugs

= Purpose of medication Drugs can be administered for these purposes

- Diagnostic purpose: to identify any disease

• Prophylaxis: to prevent the occurrence of disease. eg:- heparin to prevent thrombosis or antibiotics to prevent infection.

• Therapeutic purpose : to cure the disease.

Q 5. Responsibilities of Nurses Regarding Drug Administration

= **Responsibilities of Nurses Regarding Drug Administration**

• Nurses are both legally and morally responsible for correct administration of medications.They must: • Follow institutional policy. • Consider clients' desires and abilities. • Foster compliance. • Correctly document all actions related to medication administration and medication errors.

Nursing Responsibilities in Medication Administration

Be knowledgeable about medications being administered and being taken by the patient

Know what to do in the event of an adverse reaction

Verify and clarify orders that seem inappropriate

Be knowledgeable and informed concerning agency policies, especially concerning JCAHO's National Patient Safety Goals

Follow standards of nursing practice

Observe standard precautions and use medical-surgical asepsis if indicated

Confirm "7 rights" of safe medication administration

Document medication delivery and patient response accurately and appropriately

Report adverse events or incidents per agency policy

Q 6 . Enlist factors influencing drug action

= FACTORS AFFECTING

MEDICATION ACTION

A number of factors other than the drug itself can affect its action. A

person may not respond in the same manner to successive doses of a

drug. In addition, the identical drug and dosage may affect different

clients differently.

Developmental Factors :

During pregnancy women must be very careful about taking medications. Drugs taken during pregnancy pose a risk throughout the pregnancy, but pose the highest risk during the first trimester, due to the

formation of vital organs and functions of the fetus during this time.

Infants usually require small dosages because of their body size and the immaturity of their organs, especially the liver and kidneys.

gs formerly tolerated. Older adults have different responses to medications due to physiological changes that accompany aging. These changes include decreased liver and kidney function, which can result in the accumulation of the drug in the body

Older adults often experience decreased gastric motility and decreased gastric acid production and blood flow, which can impair drug absorption

Gender :

Differences in the way men and women respond to drugs are chiefly

related to the distribution of body fat and fluid and hormonal differences. Because most drug research is done on men, more research on

women is required to reflect the effects of hormonal changes on drug

actions in women.

Cultural, Ethnic, and Genetic Factors :

A client's response to a drug is influenced by genetic variations such

as gender, size, and body composition. This variation in response is

called pharmacogenetics, a branch of pharmacology that examines the role of genetics in drug response.

Diet :

Nutrients can affect the action of a medication. For example,

vitamin K, found in green leafy vegetables, can counteract the effect

of an anticoagulant such as warfarin

Environment :

The client's environment can affect the action of drugs, particularly

those used to alter behavior and mood

Environmental temperature may also affect drug activity. When environmental temperature is high, the peripheral blood vessels dilate, thus intensifying the action of vasodilators.

Psychological Factors

A client's expectations about what a drug can do can affect the response to the medication. For example, a client who believes that codeine is ineffective as an analgesic may experience no relief from pain

after it is given.

Illness and Disease

Illness and disease can also affect the action of drugs. For example,

aspirin can reduce the body temperature of a feverish client but has

no effect on the body temperature of a client without fever. Drug action is altered in clients with circulatory, liver, or kidney dysfunction.

Time of Administration

The time of administration of oral medications affects the relative speed with which they act. Some orally administered medications are absorbed more quickly if the stomach is empty, whereas other medications have a more rapid absorption when administered with food.

CHAPTER THIRTEEN

UNIT 13: POSTOPERATIVE UNIT

SHORT ANSWER QUESTION

Q 1. Postoperative care

= INTRODUCTION

The post operative period begins from the time the patient leaves the operating room and ends with the follow up visit by the surgeon. The post operative care is provided by - PACU and SICU.

PHASES OF POST OP UNIT Two phases- Phase I & Phase II

Phase I - It is the immediate recovery phase and requires intensive nursing care to detect early signs of complication. Receive a complete patient record from the operating room which to plan post operative care. It is designated for care of surgical patient immediately after surgery and patient requiring close monitoring.

Phase II = Care of the surgical patient who has been transferred from the Phase I post op unit.

Patient requiring less observation and less nursing care than Phase I

This phase is also known as Step down or progressive care unit.

NURSING MANAGEMENT IN POST OP UNIT

To provide care until the patient has recovered from the effect of anesthesia. Assessing the patient Monitor vitals-pulse volume and regularity, depth and nature of respiration. Assessment of patient's O2 saturation. Skin colour.

ASSESSMENT OF THE SURGICAL SITE

Haemorrhage It is a serious complication of surgery that resulting death.

It can occur in immediate post operatively or upto several days after surgery.

If left untreated,cardiac output decreases and blood pressure and Hb level will fall rapidly.

Discharge from the Post Operative

Unit A patient remains in the post op unit, untill the patient has fully recoverd from anesthesia. Following measures are used to determine the patient ready for disharge from post operative unit.

Stable vital signs

Orientation to Person Place Time or events

Adequate oxygen saturation level.

Urine out put at least 30ml/hour

Minimal pain.

Adequate respiratory function.

Aldrete score more than ‘ 9 ‘ before shifting from Post Operative Anaesthesia Care Unit

Q 2. Principles of bandaging.

= **Defination** : A strip of material used mainly to support and immobilize a part of the body. Bandaging is the process of covering a wound or an injured part.

USES:

? To prevent contamination of wound by holding dressings in position.

? To provide support to the part that is injured, sprained or dislocated joint.

? To provide rest to the part that is injured.

? To prevent and control hemorrhage.

? To restrict movement / immobilize a fracture or a dislocation.

? To correct deformity.

? To maintain pressure.

GENERAL PRINCIPLES:

? Wash hands. (Wear gloves where necessary). Select a bandage of proper size & suitable material. Put the patient in a comfortable position. Support the injured area while bandaging. If a joint is involved, flex it slightly. Face the patient while applying the bandage, except when applying it to the head.

? Hold the roll of the bandage in the right hand when applying bandage on the left side, Hold the bandage with the roll uppermost and apply the outer surface to the skin, unrolling a few centimeters of the bandage at a time. Put some cotton wool on the part to be bandaged so that the bandage does not slip or cause cutting into the skin underneath. Bandage from below upward, and from within outward.

? Hold the end of the of the bandage over the outer aspect of the injured area and wind the bandage around the part twice to fix it. When bandaging a limb start with an oblique turn to keep the bandage in position, as an alternative method. Cover two thirds of the bandage by the next one, while covering a large area by winding the roller bandage around the part. Keep the edges parallel. Keep even and not too tight pressure while applying bandage, too tight bandage interferes with circulation.

? Finish with a straight turn and fix the end with a safety pin, sticking plaster or by dividing the terminal portion of the bandage longitudinally and tying the two ends around the bandaged part. If possible, leave fingers and toes exposed to check circulation. Do not bandage the part too tightly or too loosely. Observe the extremities carefully for any signs of swelling or blueness due to interference with circulation by a bandage that is too tight. When removing a bandage, pass it from one hand to the other, so that it is collected in a concertina fashion.

Principles & Procedures for applying Bandages

- Wash hands. (Wear gloves where necessary)
- Assist victim to assume comfortable position on bed or chair and support the body part to be bandaged.
- Always stand in front of the part/victim to be bandaged except when applying a bandage to the head, eye and ear.
- Be sure the bandage is rolled firm.
- Make sure the body part to be bandaged is clean and dry.
- Assess skin before applying bandage for any breakdown.
- Observe circulation by noting pulse, surface temperature, skin color and sensation of the body part to be wrapped.

Principles & Procedures for applying Bandages (contd.

- Always start bandaging from inner to outer far to near end.
- When bandaging a joint, ensures flexibility (except if immobilization of joint is requirec
- Always start and end with two circular turn
- Cover the area 2 inches above and 2 inch affected area (wound).
- Overlap turns and slightly stretch the band
- Cover two third 2/3 of the previous turn.
- Where possible, leave fingertips or toe tips observation (adequacy of blood circulation
- End the bandage on the outer side of the b end a bandage on wound or at the back of

Principales of Bandaging

Q 3. METHODS OF APPLYING BANDAGES

= **DEFINITION:** A strip of material used mainly to support and immobilize a part of the body. Bandaging is the process of covering a wound or an injured part.

USES: ? To prevent contamination of wound by holding dressings in position. ? To provide support to the part that is injured, sprained or dislocated joint. ? To provide rest to the part that is injured. ? To prevent and control hemorrhage. ? To restrict movement / immobilize a fracture or a dislocation. ? To correct deformity. ? To maintain pressure.

1. Circular turns are used chiefly to anchor bandages and to terminate bandages. ? Apply the end of the bandage to the part of the body to be bandaged. ? Encircle the body part a few times or as needed, each turn directly covering the pervious turn. ? Secure the end of the bandage with tape, metal clips or a safety pin over an uninjured area.

2. Spiral turns are used to bandage cylindrical parts of the body that are fairly uniform in circumference, such as upper arm and upper leg. ? Make two circular turns to begin the bandage. ? Continue spiral turns at about a 30-degree angle, each turn overlapping the preceding one by twothirds the width of the bandage. ? Terminate the bandage with two circular turns, and secure the end as described for circular turns.

3. Spiral reverse turns are used to bandage cylindrical parts of the body that are not uniform in circumference, such as the lower leg or lower forearm. ? Begin the bandage with two circular turns, and bring the bandage upward at about a 30-degree angle. ? Place the thumb of the free hand on the upper edge of the bandage. ? The thumb will hold the bandage while it is folded on it self. ? Unroll the bandage about 4-6 then turn the hand so that the bandage is folded down. ? Continue the bandage around the limb, overlapping each previous turn by two-thirds the width of the bandage. ? Make each bandage turn at the same position on the limb so that the turns of the bandage will be aligned. ? Terminate the bandage with two circular turns, and secure the end as described for circular turns.

4. The figure-of-eight method permits flexibility of the elbow, knee and ankle without disturbing the dressing. ? Begin the bandage with two circular turns. ? Carry the bandage above the joint, around it, and then below it, making a figure eight-continue above and below the joint, overlapping the previous turn by two-thirds the width of the bandage. ? Terminate the bandage above the joint with two circular turns, and secure the end appropriately.

5. Head bandaging: Vertical bandage carried twice forwards and once backwards. Continue to pass the vertical bandage backwards and forwards, each time a little to the left and right alternately,

locking it with the horizontal bandage. Finally, pass horizontal bandage twice around the head, and pin in front.

6. Triangular Bandage to the Head: ? Turn the base (longest side) of the bandage up and center its base on center of the forehead, letting the point (apex) fall on the back of the neck. ? Take the ends behind the head and cross the ends over the apex. ? Take them over the forehead and tie them. ? Tuck the apex behind the crossed part of the bandage and/or secure it with a safety pin, if available.

7. Eye Injury & Bandaging A penetrating eye injury is usually caused by a sharp object which has gone in, or is protruding from the eye. ? Support casualty's head to keep it as still as possible. ? Ask casualty to try not to move eyes. ? Place sterile pad or dressing over injured eye. ? Ask casualty to hold this in place. ? Bandage dressing in place, covering injured eye. ? If penetrating eye injury, lie casualty on back, place pad around object and bandage in place. Warning: ? Do not touch the eye or any contact lens. ? Do not allow casualty to rub eye. ? Do not try to remove any object which is penetrating the eye. ? Do not apply pressure when bandaging the eye.

8. Ear bandage: ? Lay the outer surface of the bandage against forehead and carry the bandage round the head in one circular turn, bandaging away from the injured ear. ? Towards the sound side, carry the bandage round to the back of the head, low down in the nape of the neck again, repeat these. ? Each turn being slightly higher than the previous one as it cover the dressing, but slightly over as it cover the hair. ? Continue until the whole is covered and complete the bandage by one straight turn around the forehead, pinning where all the turns cross one another some people prefer to take the bandage around the forehead between each turn covering the dressing, but this makes a heavy bulk around the head which is not really necessary.

9. Jaw Injuries and Bandaging: ? Remove all foreign material from the casualty's mouth. ? If the casualty is unconscious, check for obstructions in the airway. ? When applying the bandage, allow the jaw enough freedom to permit passage of air and drainage from

the mouth. ? Place the bandage under the chin and carry its ends upward. Adjust the bandage to make one end longer than the other. ? Take the longer end over the top of the head to meet the short end at the temple and cross the ends over. ? Take the ends in opposite directions to the other side of the head and tie them over the part of the bandage that was applied first.

10. Apply a Triangular Bandage Sling: A triangular bandage sling is usually made from a muslin bandage, but any material that does not stretch (such as a fatigue shirt, trousers, poncho, blanket, or shelter-half) can be used. Fold, cut, or tear the material into a triangular shape. ? Insert the material under the injured arm so that the arm is in the center, the apex of the sling is beyond the elbow, and the top corner of the material is over the shoulder of the injured side. ? Position the forearm so that the hand is slightly higher than the elbow (about a 10 degree angle). ? Bring the lower portion of the material over the injured arm so that the bottom corner goes over the shoulder of the uninjured side. ? Bring the top corner behind the casualty's neck. ? Tie the two corners together so that the knot will not slip. The knot should fit into the & quot; hollow" at the side of the neck on the uninjured side.

Q 3 .Golden rules for bandaging

= Golden rules for bandaging

a) Wash hands. Be careful not to spread contamination via hair or wound debris.

Remember also to wash hands thoroughly after finishing the dressing.

b) Collect all materials together, placed within easy reach, including scissors, soapy wash if needed, new dressings, bandages and other essential equipment.

c) If removing a soiled dressing, dispose of it quickly and safely into a clinical waste bag, likewise with all cotton wool and swabs used to clean the wound.

d) If bandaging the lower limb, it is advisable to include the foot in the bandage.

This will help prevent swelling. Pressure points and extremities should be padded

out first.

e) If bandaging extremities, start from the distal end to prevent pocketing of blood.

f) Only unroll a small amount of bandage at a time. This will enable a more even

tension to be applied throughout. It will also be easier to handle. Reverse roll

bandage on to the patient wherever possible.

g) Apply bandage firmly, with ½ to $^{2}/3$ overlap in a spiral action. Be careful not to

apply too tightly (especially elasticated bandages) as this will impede circulation,

but firmly enough to perform the desired requirement and to ensure that they

will not fall off.

h) Avoid sticking bandages to the animal's skin or hair except where bandaging tails

for example, where hair may need to be included to hold the bandage on.

i) If bandaging a fractured limb, include joints above and below fracture as

appropriate. Likewise, pad out pressure points, e.g. hock and elbow, as required.

This will necessitate incorporating the foot to prevent distal oedema, but will

depend on the site of the fracture.

j) Where necessary, secure ends of bandage either by splitting and tying in a reef

knot, or adhesive tape. Do not use clips, pins or elastic bands.

k) Choose your bandages carefully. Ensure the correct type for the correct

usage. Similarly, choose an appropriate width. Too wide and the edges may be cumbersome and could roll over, too narrow and it may cause stringing and

become uncomfortable for the patient. Likewise, it will ease your application if

the correct bandage has been chosen for the appropriate job.

CHAPTER FOURTEEN

UNIT 14: MEETING SPECIAL NEEDS OF THE PATIENT

SHORT ANSWER QUESTION

Q 1. Care of unconscious patient

= CONSCIOUSNESS

- A state of awareness of yourself and your surroundings
- Ability to perceive sensory stimuli and respond appropriately to them.

Abnormal state - client is unarousable and unresponsive.

- Coma is a deepest state of unconsciousness.
- Unconsciousness is a symptom rather than a disease.

Degrees of unconsciousness that vary in length and severity:

- Brief – fainting
- Prolonged – deep coma
- **Unconsciousness** is when a person is unable to respond to people and activities.
- A person may become unconscious due to oxygen deprivation, shock, central nervous system depressants such as alcohol and

drugs, or injury.

-
- **DEFINITION**
- Interruption of awareness of oneself and one's surroundings, lack of the ability to notice or respond to stimuli in the environment.

Sign and Symptom

- The person will be unresponsive (does not respond to activity, touch, sound, or other stimulation
- Is unaware of his surroundings and does not respond to sound
- Makes no purposeful movements
- Does not respond to questions or to touch
- Drowsiness
- Inability to speak or move parts of his or her body
- Loss of bowel or bladder control (incontinence)
- Stupor

Level of consciousness

1. **Alert:** Normal consciousness.
2. **Alertness, oriented:** opens eyes continuously, respond to stimuli appropriately.
3. **Lethargy, sleepy:** slow to respond but appropriate response, open eyes to stimuli
4. **Stupor:** aroused by and opens eyes to painful stimuli, never fully awake , confused, unclear conversation.
5. **Semi-coma Stage:** moves in response to painful stimuli, no conversation, protective blinking/swallowing , papillary reflex present.
6. **Coma:** unresponsive except to severe pain, no protective reflexes, fixed pupils, no voluntary movements.

Care to be given to unconscious patient : Nsg. Aims: - • Identify problems. • Prevent secondry complications. • Maximise functional recovery. • Support patient and relatives.

Care of unconscious Pt: - • Emg. Management: - ABC. • Air – way clearance: - suctioning / positioning. • Prevention of risk of injury: - – Altered cognitive status. – Strain, padding and support. – Side rails, foot splint / board. • Maintanance of fluid volume: - – I/O, IVF, N/G feeding, orally. • Care of oral cavity – mouth care 4 hrly. • Maintain tissue integrity of cornea: - abscent corneal reflex, eye care, pad.

Prevention from cold: - – Damage of hypothalamic center. – Warm clothing / protection. • Catheter care / VS urinary care. – Incontinence care, – Catheterized. – Retention care, – Stimulation intemittat – Catheterization, folly's. • Bowel care: - • Constipation care – fluid / fiber / laxatives. • Diarrhea – fluid / ors. • Impaction – digital removal.

• Prevention of pressure ulcer: - • Back care, positioning, air / water matters etc. • Skin care: - Positioning, bed bath, hair wash, nail. • Nutritional care: - N/G, TPN, IVF, I/O. • Pyrexia: - room cold, ventilation, TPR, cold. • Promoting sensory stimulation: - – To prevent from sensory deprivation. Care: - Touching the Pt., communicating with Pt., avoid negative comments near Pt., Orient Pt. about: time, place, person ev.8 hrly. Divertional therapy: radio, music etc. • Monitoring and managing potential comp: - e.g. Pneumonia, aspiration, respiratory failure. Care: - TPR, BP, blood count, ABG, suctioning, chest physio., C/S – blood and secretions.

Q 2. Non pharmacological management of pain

= Non-pharmacological therapies are typically categorized into

1 Physical (sensory) interventions

Physical (sensory) interventions typically are patient-specific and inhibit nociceptive input and pain perception. Some measures that can reduce pain intensity and improve the patient quality of life such as massage, positioning, hot and cold treatment, transcutaneous electrical nerve stimulation (TENS), acupuncture and progressive muscle relaxation.

2. **Psychological interventions** Continuous pain may lead to development of maladaptive status and behavior that worsen day to day function, increase distress, or enhancing the experience of pain. Patients suffering pain tend to show increased vulnerability to a variety of psychiatric illnesses, including depressive and anxiety disorders, and posttraumatic stress disorder. In fact, the relationship between depression and pain is likely to be bidirectional, so that the presence of a depressive disorder has been identified as a key risk factor in the transition from acute to chronic pain. Most commonly used psychological interventions are: cognitive behavioral therapy, mindfulness-based stress reduction, acceptance and commitment therapy (ACT), guided imagery and biofeedback.

3. **Others Spirituality and religion in pain management and music therapy.**

2. Physical (sensory) interventions

2.1. **Massage**

Pain can complicate the patient condition as it can elevate stress, altering posture, and reduce one's ability to participate in daily activity [1]. It is the process of rubbing and kneading parts of the body, especially joints and muscles with hands to relieve pain and decrease tension. Massage can interrupt the patient's cycle of distress. It can increase the blood circulation as well as lymphatic circulation. Massage can also initiate an analgesic effect to the area being rubbed and decrease inflammation and edema. Moreover, it can release muscle spasms manually while increasing endogenous endorphin release, and conflicting sensory stimuli that override pain signals.

2. **Positioning Positioning** is a physical intervention that includes maintaining a proper body alignment to reduce stress and anxiety, especially in children. It helps to prevent further complications, reduces the risk for developing injuries, prevents developing bed ulcers and most importantly reduce alleviate pain. Therefore, positioning the

patient correctly and re-positioning can help with the above complications

Positioning can help with many patients as it can relieve muscle pain, tension and discomfort. It can improve blood circulation which in turn prevents ulcers from developing. Moreover, elevating extremities while positioning can be beneficial in decreasing pain and prevent edema as well.

3. **Hot and cold Several** studies have shown reduction in pain, anxiety, nausea and heart rate in patients treated with active warming for pain related to mild trauma, cystitis, urolithiasis, cholelithiasis, appendicitis, colitis, and rectal trauma. This is an inexpensive and easy-to-use therapy with minimal side effects when used appropriately. Cold therapy includes applying a cool substance or device to any part of the body. Numerous studies have reported that cold treatment can increase pain threshold, decrease edema, and suppress the inflammatory process.

Cold compresses may be used between 15 and 30 min time periods and up to 2–3 times per day. Hot and cold therapy has been used for many decades and centuries to relieve pain, which includes muscle pain, joints pain, extremities pain, back pain and arthritis. Some studies show evidence that ice and heat therapies are effective and can reduce pain when compared to over the counter meds such as Paracetamol and Ibuprofen.

4. **Acupuncture** This has been used for around 5000 years, and it is considered one of the world's oldest arts of an empiric body healing. Basically, acupuncture works by putting the needle in specific region of the body, which stimulates the nerve. Each needle will cause no discomfort to little discomfort to the patient, but it will produce a small injury at the insertion area which will stimulate the body and the

immune system to increase circulation, wound healing, pain modulation and pain analgesia

2.5. Transcutaneous electrical nerve stimulation

Transcutaneous electrical nerve stimulation (TENS) is an electrical device used to treat pain.

It consists of battery-powered unit and has 2–4 leads connected to sticky pads, which are

positioned over the skin to cover or surround the painful area.

The TENS unit delivers a low-voltage electrical impulse to the padded surface electrodes in a

series of alternating electrical current impulses.

The larger impulses are postulated to activate large myelinated fibers.

5. **Progressive muscle relaxation** Progressive muscle relaxation is a technique where the participant involved tightens and relaxes different muscle groups throughout the body in a progressive manner that would provoke a sense of relaxation and comfort.

3. Psychological interventions

3.1. Cognitive behavioral therapy Incorporating the biopsychosocial (BPS) model to pain management by targeting cognitive responses to pain and maladaptive behavioral in addition to social and environmental factors that may play an important role in modifying reactions to pain . Such therapy has shown efficacy for many physical disorders and psychiatric illnesses, as well as pain

3.2. Mindfulness-based stress reduction This approach aims to disconnect the link between the sensory elements of pain from the emotional and evaluative elements and enhances uncoupled awareness of both somatic and psychological sensations []. Because the signal of pain usually cannot be distinguished, such detachment may alter the response to pain.

3.5. Guided imagery It is a technique in which an experienced practitioner helps a patient provoke a state of mind or mental images in the absence of that stimuli, defined by Bresler and Rossman as a range of techniques from simple visualization and direct imagery-based suggestions through metaphor and storytelling.

4. Others

4.1. Spirituality and religion In the middle ages, pain was considered a religious matter. Pain was seen as God's punishment for sins, or as evidence that an individual was possessed by demons. Spiritual counseling in such situation can be more of a priority than medical treatment [41]. Major parts of Hindu believers consider pain as a God punishment or as a result of personal actions. In Islam, it can be vindictive or Allah's willingness. A common Buddhist belief is that suffering is the price of attachment

4.2. Music therapy Music has been used since ancient times to enhance wellbeing and reduce pain and suffering. Playing music for patients during or after surgery helps reduce pain and use of morphine and other sedatives, anxiolytics, and analgesics

Q 3. NURSES ROLE IN PAIN MANAGEMENT

1. = NURSES ROLE IN PAIN MANAGEMENT: NURSING DIAGNOSIS Pain acute Self-care deficit Anxiety Ineffective coping Fatigue Impaired physical mobility Imbalanced nutrition less than body requirements Ineffective role performance Disturbed sleep pattern Sexual dysfunction Impaired social interaction
2. NURSES ROLE IN PAIN MANAGEMENT: PLANNING Goals and outcomes Ex: goal- "the client will achieve a satisfactory level of pain relief within 24 hours"; possible outcomes-" reporting that the pain is a 3 or less on scale, using pain relief measures safely" Setting priorities: Ex: pain related to incisional pain can be reduced by analgesics but pain related to early labor contractions will only reduced by relaxation excercises. Continuity of care: A comprehensive plan includes a variety

of resources for pain control which include nurse specialists, doctors of pharmacolology, physical therapist, occupational therapist.

CHAPTER FIFTEEN

UNIT 15: CARE OF TERMINALLY ILL PATIENT

SHORT ANSWER QUESTION

Q .1 Care of dying patient

= **ASSESSING NEEDS:**

- The nurse assesses the knowledge base of the client and family pertaining to the client's illness and previous care.
- She determines their perception of present situation, strength and weakness so that they can be used in planning nursing care.
- She assesses coping behaviors of client and his/her family

PSYCHOLOGICAL SUPPORT:

- There are five psychological stages that dying persons pass through. These are denial, anger, bargaining, depression and acceptance. In all these stages, nurse needs to be truthful but prudent in all their dealing with patient to be warm supportive and understanding.
- Develop such relation that let the patient tell you what he knows about his condition.
- Try to use his own words when talking to him. The psychological needs of a dying person can be summarized as follows:

- Relief from loneliness, fear and depression
- Maintenance of security, self confidence and dignity
- Maintenance of hope
- Meeting the spiritual needs according to his religious customs

SYMPTOMATIC MANAGEMENT:

a. **Problems associated with breathing:**

- Oxygen inhalation may be given to ease his discomfort
- Elevation of patients head and shoulders may make breathing easier
- Keep the room well ventilated and keep crowd away
- Periodic suctioning is necessary in order to maintain patency of airway
- Change position frequently atleast 2 hourly

b) Problems associated with eating and drinking:

- Anorexia, nausea and vomiting are commonly seen problems in the dying persons. They may be unable to swallow even the sips of water.
- I/V fluids should be given
- If they can tolerate oral fluids, sips of fluids should be given
- Maintain frequent oral hygiene frequently
- Apply emollients to dry lips
- Dentures should be removed and kept safely

c) Problems associated with elimination:

- Constipation, retention of urine and incontinence of urine and stools are some of the problems faced by the patient.
- Each problem should be prevented or atleast treated if possible

d) Problems associated with immobility:

- Patients should be comfortably placed and their position frequently changed in bed.
- Frequent skin care should be done to prevent the pressure ulcers

e) Problems associated with sense organs:

- Since the patient loses sight, so before giving any care to patient the nurses should touch the patient and speak appropriate words
- Avoid any type of whispering before the patient

f) Problems associated with rest and sleep:

- All the possible care should be given to the patient for alleviating pain and discomfort. Patient should not be disturbed when sleeping.

g)Problems associated with cleanliness and grooming:

- Cleanliness and appearance are important until the last breath end.
- Cleanliness of skin, care of hair, care of mouth, clean clothing are also very important

Q 2. Care of terminally ill patient

= Terminal illness is a disease that cannot be cured or adequately treated and that is reasonably expected to result in the death of the patient within a short period of time. This term is more commonly used for progressive diseases such as cancer or advanced heart disease than for trauma.

- **Hospice** care is a type of care and philosophy of care that focuses on the palliation of a chronically ill, terminally ill or seriously ill patient's pain and symptoms, and attending to their emotional and spiritual needs.

- Hospice care seeks to improve the quality of life and wellbeing of adults and children with a life-limiting or terminal illness, helping them live as fully as they can for the precious time they have
- left. It aspires to be accessible to all who could benefit and reflect personal preferences and needs.
- The modern concept of hospice includes palliative care for the incurably ill given in such institutions as hospitals or nursing homes, but also care provided to those who would rather spend their last months and days of life in their own homes.
- The first modern hospice care was created by Cicely Saunders in 1967.
- Hospice care is for people with a life expectancy of 6 months or less (if the illness runs its normal course). If you live longer than 6 months, you can still get hospice care, as long as the hospice medical director or other hospice doctor recertifies that you're terminally ill.
- Hospice care is appropriate when a person will no longer benefit from curative treatment and life expectancy is approximately six months if the disease runs its normal course.
- Hospice care is free for everyone, and is provided for however long it is needed, which could be days, weeks or even months.

- **Hospice services**

- Hospices provide a range of services which include:
- pain and symptom control
- psychological and social support
- rehabilitation
- complementary therapies, such as massage and aromatherapy
- counselling
- spiritual care
- practical and financial advice
- support in bereavement.

Q 3 . Stages of grieving by Kubler Ross.

=

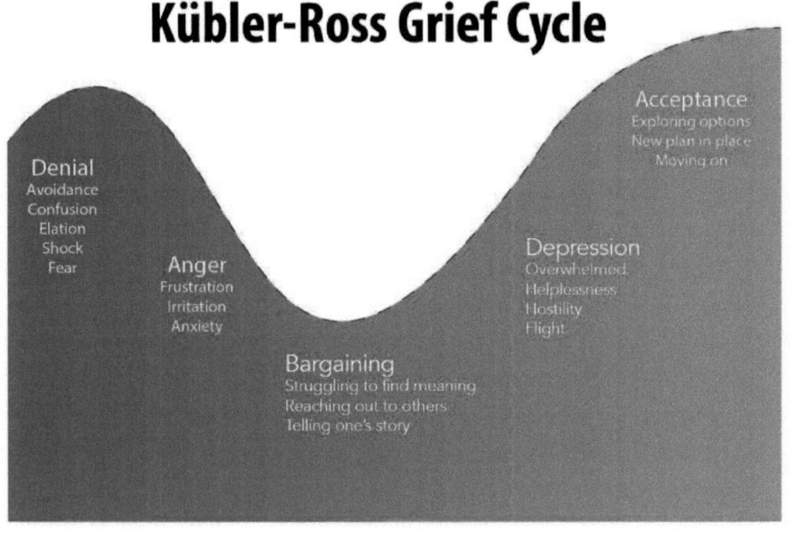

Stages of grieving by Kubler Ross

Stage of Grief	Clinical Definition
Denial	A conscious or unconscious decision to refuse to admit that something is true; in patients with diabetic foot disease, this could be the diagnosis of diabetes, sequelae of the disease process, the severity of a clinical situation, or the need for a recommended intervention Several forms of denial exist, including denial of fact, impact, awareness, cycle, and denial
Anger	An emotional or physical act in which the patient attempts to place blame Patients often report a lack of trust with their treating physician Physicians themselves could develop anger as a response
Bargaining	A negotiative process in which patients attempt to postpone or distance themselves from the reality of a situation
Depression	A feeling of loss of control or hopelessness with a situation Diabetic patients are more likely to experience depression, and depressed diabetic patients are more likely to undergo amputation
Acceptance	A feeling of stability or resignation as the patient becomes an active participant in their life

Stages of grieving by Kubler Ross

CHAPTER SIXTEEN

UNIT 16: PROFESSIONAL NURSING CONCEPTS AND PRACTICES

SHORT ANSWER QUESTION

Q 1. Health belief model

= The **health belief model** (HBM) is a social psychological health behavior change model developed to explain and predict health-related behaviors, particularly in regard to the uptake of health services. The HBM was developed in the 1950s by social psychologists at the U.S. Public Health Service and remains one of the best known and most widely used theories in health behavior research. The HBM suggests that people's beliefs about health problems, perceived benefits of action and barriers to action, and self-efficacy explain engagement (or lack of engagement) in health-promoting behavior. A stimulus or cue to action, must also be present in order to trigger the health-promoting behavior.

Perceived susceptibility

Perceived susceptibility refers to subjective assessment of risk of developing a health problem. The HBM predicts that individuals who perceive that they are susceptible to a particular health problem will engage in behaviors to reduce their risk of developing the health problem

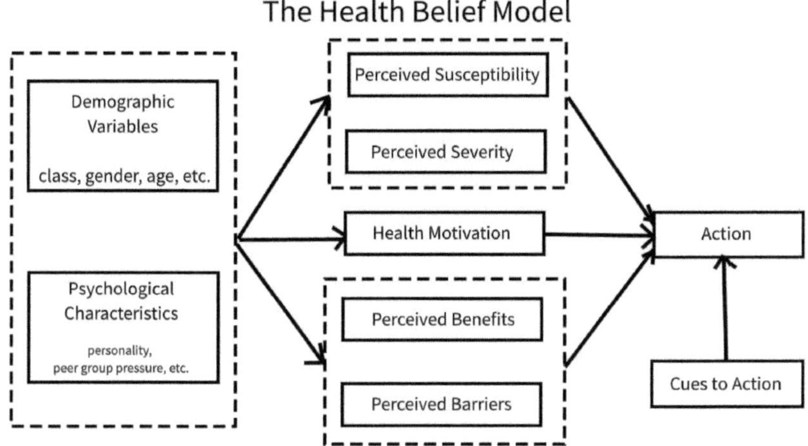

Perceived severity[

Perceived severity refers to the subjective assessment of the severity of a health problem and its potential consequences. The HBM proposes that individuals who perceive a given health problem as serious are more likely to engage in behaviors to prevent the health problem from occurring (or reduce its severity)

Perceived benefits[

Health-related behaviors are also influenced by the perceived benefits of taking action.[6] Perceived benefits refer to an individual's assessment of the value or efficacy of engaging in a health-promoting behavior to decrease risk of disease

Perceived barriers

Health-related behaviors are also a function of perceived barriers to taking action.] Perceived barriers refer to an individual's assessment of the obstacles to behavior change.] Even if an individual perceives a health condition as threatening and believes that a particular action will effectively reduce the threat, barriers may prevent engagement in the health-promoting behavior. In other words, the perceived benefits must outweigh the perceived barriers in order for behavior change to occur.

Q 2. Define theory. Discuss metaparadigms of nursing. Explain Orem's nursing theory.

= **Define . a formal statement of the rules on which a subject of study is based or of ideas that are suggested to explain a fact or event or, more generally, an opinion or explanation.**

THE METAPARADIGM FOR NURSING

In the late 20th century, much of the theoretical work in nursing focused on articulating relationships among four major concepts: person, environment, health, and nursing. Because these four concepts

can be superimposed on almost any work in nursing, they are collectively referred to as the metaparadigm for nursing. The term originates from two Greek words: meta, meaning "with," and paradigm,

meaning "pattern." Many consider the following four concepts to be

central to nursing:

1. The individuals or **clients** are the recipients of nursing care (includes individuals, families, groups, and communities).
2. The **environment** is the internal and external surroundings that

affect the client. This includes people in the physical environment, such as families, friends, and significant others.

3. **Health** is the degree of wellness or well-being that the client experiences.
4. **Nursing** is the attributes, characteristics, and actions of the nurse

providing care on behalf of, or in conjunction with, the client.

Orem's General Theory of Nursing

Dorothea Orem's theory, first published in 1971, includes three related concepts: self-care, self-care deficit, and nursing systems. Self-care theory is based on four concepts: self-care, self-care agency, self-care requisites, and therapeutic self-care demand. Self-care refers to those activities an individual performs independently throughout life to promote and maintain personal well-being. Self-care agency is the individual's ability to perform self-care activities. It consists of two agents: a self-care agent (an individual who performs self-care independently) and a dependent care agent (a person other than the individual who provides the care). Most adults care for themselves, whereas infants and people weakened by illness or disability require assistance with self-care activities.

Self-care requisites, also called self-care needs, are measures or actions taken to provide self-care. There are three categories of selfcare requisites:

1. Universal requisites are common to all people. They include maintaining intake and elimination of air, water, and food; balancing rest, solitude, and social interaction; preventing hazards to life and well-being; and promoting normal human functioning.

2. Developmental requisites result from maturation or are associated with conditions or events, such as adjusting to a change in body image or to the loss of a spouse.

3. Health deviation requisites result from illness, injury, or disease or its treatment. They include actions such as seeking health care assistance, carrying out prescribed therapies, and learning to live with the effects of illness or treatment.

Therapeutic self-care demand refers to all self-care activities required to meet existing self-care requisites, or in other words, actions to maintain health and well-being.

Self-care deficit results when self-care agency is not adequate to meet the known self-care demand. Orem's self-care deficit theory explains not only when nursing is needed but also how people can be assisted through five methods of helping: acting or doing for, guiding,

teaching, supporting, and providing an environment that promotes
the individual's abilities to meet current and future demands.

Orem identifies three types of nursing systems. The five methods of helping discussed for self-care deficit can be used in each of the
three nursing systems:

1. Wholly compensatory systems are required for individuals who
are unable to control and monitor their environment and process information.

2. Partly compensatory systems are designed for individuals who
are unable to perform some, but not all, self-care activities.

3. Supportive-educative (developmental) systems are designed for
persons who need to learn to perform self-care measures and need assistance to do so.

Q 3. Discuss Peplau's theory and its implication to nursing.

= Peplau's Interpersonal Relations Model

Hildegard Peplau, a psychiatric nurse, introduced her interpersonal
concepts in 1952. Central to Peplau's theory is the existence of a therapeutic relationship between the nurse and the client. Nurses enter
into a personal relationship with an individual when a need is present. The nurse–client relationship evolves in four phases:

1. Orientation. The client seeks help and the nurse assists the client
to understand the problem and the extent of the need for help.

2. Identification. The client assumes a posture of dependence,
interdependence, or independence in relation to the nurse (relatedness). The nurse's focus is on ensuring the individual that
the nurse understands the interpersonal meaning of the client's situation.

3. Exploitation. The client derives full value from what the nurse offers through the relationship. The client uses available services based on self-interest and needs. Power shifts from the nurse to the client.

4. Resolution. In the final phase, old needs and goals are put aside and new ones adopted. Once older needs are resolved, newer and more mature ones emerge.

To help clients fulfill their needs, nurses assume many roles: stranger, teacher, resource person, surrogate, leader, and counselor.

Peplau's model continues to be used by clinicians when working with individuals who have psychological problems............

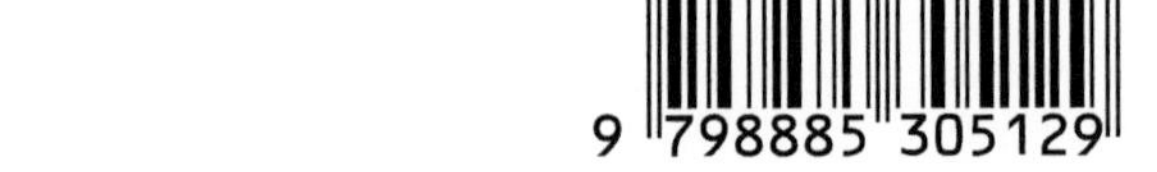

Printed by Libri Plureos GmbH in Hamburg,
Germany